Workplace Safety and Health

Workplace Safety and Health

The Role of Workers' Compensation

James Robert Chelius

American Enterprise Institute for Public Policy Research
Washington, D.C.

James Robert Chelius teaches industrial relations and labor economics at the Krannert Graduate School of Management, Purdue University, West Lafayette, Indiana.

Library of Congress Cataloging in Publication Data

Chelius, James Robert.
    Workplace safety and health.

    (AEI studies ; 174)
    Includes bibliographical references.
    1. Workmen's compensation—United States. I.   Title.
II.   Series: American Enterprise Institute for Public
Policy Research.   AEI studies ; 174.
KF3615.C5   344'.73'021   77-21085

ISBN 0–8447–3274–5

AEI Studies 174

Printed in the United States of America

CONTENTS

INTRODUCTION

Regulation of industrial safety, which began in the late nineteenth century, was one of the earliest government constraints on business. The vast majority of this regulation was at the state level with little change or federal involvement. After a flurry of regulatory initiatives in the first two decades of the twentieth century, the matter received little public attention for many years, largely because of the substantial decrease in injury rates between 1920 and the early 1960s. There was no obvious need for alternative solutions since there did not appear to be a serious problem.

During the 1960s, however, injury rates began to rise. With this reversal came a renewed interest in governmental regulation of industrial safety, culminating in the passage of the Occupational Safety and Health Act of 1970 (OSHA). The act instituted a massive federal effort to regulate occupational safety and health using compulsory safety rules. It created a new federal bureaucracy charged with developing and enforcing detailed workplace safety practices. This form of regulation is obviously regarded by Congress as the primary means for overseeing industrial safety, but the act went further. It established a National Commission on State Workmen's Compensation Laws to investigate the workers' compensation system—a set of state laws that require businesses to provide cash benefits, medical care, and rehabilitation to workers injured on the job regardless of who caused the accident or disease. The National Commission was charged with examining the role of the workers' compensation system in the overall pattern of government safety regulation. It recommended a substantial increase in the employers' liability for workers' accident costs and called for a larger federal role in administering the program. Enactment of recent Congressional proposals would also substantially change the workers' compensation system.

This study examines workers' compensation as a part of our public policy toward industrial accidents and disease. We first consider the nature of the work-injury problem and of the current workers' compensation system. Traditional alternatives to workers' compensation are then explored, and suggested reforms are analyzed. The final chapter offers an alternative reform that combines the best features of the traditional alternatives and, in the author's view, overcomes the weaknesses of other proposed measures.

This study contends that neither the existing system nor the suggested reforms recognizes the dual nature of the problem. An effective solution must seek both efficient injury prevention and the provision of income security for injured workers. Unfortunately, there is a conflict between these two goals. The current system, by its nearly total concentration on income security, has disrupted the potential a liability system such as workers' compensation has for encouraging safety. The recently suggested reforms would only accentuate this concentration on income security. It is the task of any policy reform to maximize the combined achievement of both objectives rather than maximize the achievement of one while disregarding the other. The reform proposed in the final chapter combines features of the current workers' compensation system with a very limited use of court proceedings to determine fault. In this manner it provides both reasonably efficient injury prevention and substantial income security.

1
THE OCCUPATIONAL SAFETY AND HEALTH PROBLEM

The Nature of the Problem

One of every ten workers in private industry each year suffers the effects of an accident or disease incurred while working.[1] Only one-third of these incidents involve lost worktime, but lost time totals over 31 million days per year in the United States.[2] Naturally, these accidents and diseases have aroused public concern.

Without slighting the seriousness of the work-injury problem, it is helpful to place it in perspective by considering other activities which give rise to similar harm. The National Safety Council estimates that many more deaths result from nonwork automobile accidents than from all work accidents. Accidents in the home and accidents in "public-place" activities, which include swimming and hunting, also produce more deaths than working.[3] Walter Oi has estimated that ". . . fully a third of all employed persons confront a risk of being injured on the job that is lower than the risk of living in general."[4] Thus, while work injuries are a serious concern, they do not represent a unique or isolated phenomenon. Work is simply one of many activities which yields injuries. Although there are certain aspects of work which make it different from other activities, there is much that is common to all injury-producing endeavors.

---

[1] Throughout this volume, the term *injury* will be used to cover the result of both accidents and disease.

[2] Data are from a news release by the U.S. Department of Labor, Bureau of Labor Statistics, *BLS Reports Results of Occupational Injuries and Illnesses for 1974* (Washington, D.C., 1975).

[3] National Safety Council, *Accident Facts* (1975 edition), p. 3.

[4] Walter Oi, "An Essay on Workmen's Compensation and Industrial Safety," *Supplemental Studies for the National Commission on State Workmen's Compensation Laws*, vol. 1 (Washington, D.C., 1973), p. 72.

Safety as an Economic Commodity. Although work deaths and injuries are occurrences everyone would like to eliminate, unfortunately this is not possible. Many of these accidents and diseases cannot be prevented if we also want the desirable goods, services, and incomes which accompany them. All of life's activities entail the possibility of being injured or catching a disease but people do not choose just the least risky activities. Relatively hazardous activities such as working, driving, and consuming new products are freely chosen because people feel the benefits of participation outweigh the risks. Since there are benefits as well as risks to participation in all activities, the problem of risk control can be most usefully analyzed within the economist's framework of costs and benefits.

The moral anguish associated with accidents and disease notwithstanding, it must be understood that prevention is an economic commodity. Prevention can be "produced" only by the use of scarce resources which, if not allocated to prevention, could serve other beneficial purposes. The resources used for prevention usually have an obvious economic character. For example, heavy-duty automobile bumpers, protective headgear, and safety experts use resources that could be devoted to other beneficial purposes than accident and disease prevention. Of all the resources available to us for accident prevention, the most expensive is abstaining from a risky activity. Each of us avoids many activities which could give us some form of satisfaction. However desirable the satisfaction, many of us feel that activities such as riding motorcycles or building skyscrapers are far too risky compared with the rewards of participation. The fact that there are many risky activities which we do not choose to avoid simply means that we savor the rewards of these activities more than we fear the risks.

Why Occupational Safety and Health Are Special. Although working is often no more dangerous than other activities, work risks receive attention disproportionate to their impact. To understand why, it is useful to consider how people decide whether to participate in a risky activity. This choice is often very difficult. However, people usually feel comfortable with these decisions, once made, because they did have a choice and were aware of the rewards and risks when they chose. The same decision process occurs in both work and nonwork settings, but there are substantial differences. In a nonwork situation the rewards of exposure to risk typically accrue directly to the participant. Furthermore, control over the decision is usually direct and immediate. In deciding whether to drive to the beach, an individual implicitly weighs the risks of driving against the pleasures of visiting the beach. If the anticipated pleasure outweighs the anticipated risks, the individual goes to the beach. If not he stays home.

A work situation with exactly the same risks and rewards may present a more difficult decision. Whereas the worker driving to the beach to deliver food supplies exposes himself directly to the same risks as the vacationer, the direct rewards of his drive accrue to the consumers of the food he delivers. If consumers desire the benefits created by having the food at the beach, they must pay the employee's company, and the company in turn rewards the employee. Therefore, even in an ideal situation where the company pays extra wages for exposure to risk, the rewards for such risks are more indirect than in the typical nonwork situation.

In addition, the decisions controlling individual exposure to risks in the workplace frequently have a less immediate impact than non-work decisions. An individual who considers going to the beach for his own recreation can quickly make a decision or change it if conditions change, whereas an individual in the work situation must negotiate with his employer for changes in the level of risk or benefits. An individual planning a family trip to the beach can change his mind if weather conditions change and he feels the drive is too risky. If a worker encounters such a change in driving conditions, however, he may not be able to alter his schedule to accommodate the increase in risk. A worker's recourse is to negotiate with his employer, individually or through his union, to lower the level of risk or to increase wages. If the situation is not corrected the individual may have to search for a new job. Certainly the process of bargaining with an employer or changing jobs is a more difficult and complicated method of responding to a change in the level of risk than is typical in a nonwork setting.

Another factor making work safety an object of special public attention is the availability of a relatively small group to serve as scapegoats. Employers serve this function admirably. They serve as an object of blame and scorn out of proportion to their responsibility for accidents and disease simply because there are fewer employers than employees. Just as "middlemen" are almost invariably blamed for food price increases, because there are fewer of them than there are farmers or retailers, so perhaps must employers serve as the objects to be blamed for occupational injuries. Since there is no readily available scapegoat for hunting or swimming accidents, we will probably always pay less attention to these sources of injuries than to injuries which arise from work. Thus, because the benefits of risk-taking on the job are indirect, because the immediate situation is often less controllable, and because there is a readily available group to blame, the risks of work have generated special concern. It is a difficult and sensitive issue which most people feel deserves extraordinary attention.

The Concept of Optimal Safety. Since both benefits and costs are associated with risky activities, it is desirable to balance them so as to achieve an ideal or optimal amount of risk. For each individual, this desired level of risk is one in which the value placed on benefits minus costs is at a maximum. In other words, the goal is the largest level of satisfaction net of all costs including risks. Since virtually all activities entail some degree of risk, it follows that we would not want to eliminate all risks, because this would entail avoiding all rewarding activities. What is needed is a compromising balance of prevention efforts, activity benefits, and activity risks. It is therefore desirable to have arrangements by which these trade-offs can be achieved in a manner satisfactory to the individuals who comprise our society.

The desirability of accepting some positive level of risk runs counter to many people's initial reaction to the subject. At first glance, accident and disease prevention are usually seen as an unmitigated benefit whose value is infinite. It therefore is seen as something that should not be constrained by the cost of the resources required for its accomplishment. Individuals who voice this opinion should ask themselves whether they act as if this were the value they placed on prevention. To do so, they would have to go through most of life's activities with prevention as their primary goal. Of course, very few (if any) people actually behave in this manner. However, one may place whatever value one wants on prevention. The goal, again, is to provide arrangements under which individuals may trade off risks and benefits in the manner that maximizes their personal satisfactions.

If all the costs and benefits of accidents and diseases accrued to the same person, determination of the appropriate exposure to risk would be relatively straightforward. A well-informed decision maker would participate in an activity if the value of expected benefits exceeded the value of expected costs. However, the costs and benefits of certain activities, such as work, generally accrue to different decision makers. For example, products go to customers while injuries go to workers. In these cases, it is necessary to devise mechanisms which allow the balancing of costs and benefits not directly and immediately borne by the individual participants. It follows from this that the ultimate goal of government intervention in safety and health affairs should be to facilitate the arrangements by which individuals and groups seek to achieve an optimal level of risk.

4

Many people of high purpose are offended by the expression of the occupational safety and health problem in terms of costs and benefits. However, it must be remembered that this is not a normative structure imposed by economists but a formalization of the factors which concern individuals. To ignore the cost/benefit framework does not change the nature of the problem or the attributes of possible solutions. Such avoidance simply increases the likelihood that certain features of our desires or the constraints on our desires will be ignored. The use of cost/benefit labels merely categorizes and explicitly considers factors which might otherwise be ignored. Ignoring such factors does not cause them to go away, nor does it make difficult decisions easier.

We have defined the optimal level of risk as that at which the net value of benefits over costs is at a maximum for each individual. This goal is met by continuing to reduce the incidence of accidents and disease until the costs of achieving the reduction are equal to the extra benefits derived. After the equality of marginal benefits and costs has been achieved, further reduction in accidents and diseases will cost more than it is worth, which represents a net social loss. The difficulty of translating this abstract decision process into concrete identifiable terms should not deter us from recognizing the appropriateness of optimal risk as a public policy goal. To ignore this goal, because of its abstract character, can only lead to policy decisions that waste the limited resources at our disposal. While we cannot concretely and precisely define the "ideal" incidence of accidents and diseases, we must understand the nature of the trade-offs involved and make recognition of these realities an integral part of public policy.

The Role of Public Policy

For a broad range of activities our society trusts private decision makers such as workers, consumers, unions, and firms to achieve through their interaction the desired amount of goods and services. The quantity of such varied "commodities" as travel, garbage, and books is largely determined by individuals deciding how much they care to produce and consume in view of how much is received or forgone in a trade. We rely on these decisions because, in making them, people at least implicitly balance the costs and benefits of production and consumption thus satisfying themselves while preserving freedom of choice for others. An important question to ask ourselves, therefore, is whether we can trust the decisions individuals make about the production and consumption of occupational safety and health.

Our society relies on private decisions for most commodities because the costs and benefits facing individuals are the same as the costs and benefits to society. In most cases, the optimal amount for society is simply the sum of the optimal amounts for each member of society. A problem arises, however, when the full value of either costs or benefits are not known or felt by the decision maker. If the cost which accrues to the decision maker is less than the true social cost of a product or activity, then the individual will consume or produce more than is appropriate from society's point of view since the individual is ignoring costs which others must bear. A classic example of this social cost problem is pollution. We know that, because the producers who pollute have not had to bear the total costs of polluting, their production exceeds optimal levels. Steel producers, for example, have not always borne their full costs, which include the aesthetic loss of clean waterways, ill health generated by polluted air, and extra cleaning bills for families living in the vicinity of the mills. From society's viewpoint these costs are as much a part of steel production as the costs of iron ore and coal for which steel companies pay. Because these pollution costs are not paid by steel companies, the cost of steel appears to be less than it truly is. Hence, the price of steel is less than it should be, and too much steel—and pollution—are produced.

Under certain conditions private market forces will eliminate the distortion caused by ignoring these social costs. If rights are well-defined, markets are competitive, decision makers are aware of all costs, and the costs of making and enforcing contracts are negligible, then there will be no distortions due to these social costs.[5] In the case of steel pollution, its effect on the company's neighbors would be borne by the steel producers if: (1) the neighbor was aware of the problem and its cost to him; and (2) the neighbor could bargain and enforce contracts with the steel company at negligible costs. Although few would contend that this is a likely situation, the point is important because the degree to which these conditions are met will determine the extent of the distortion in production due to the divergence between social and private costs.

In occupational safety and health, the issue is whether there are any differences in costs to decision makers and in social costs which will cause a nonoptimal amount of safety to be supplied in the absence of government regulation. A social cost problem might arise if the party bearing the costs of accident prevention is not the one who

---

[5] Ronald Coase, "The Problem of Social Cost," *Journal of Law and Economics*, vol. 3 (October 1960), pp. 1-44.

receives all the benefits of prevention. In many situations, the worker receives most of the benefits of accident prevention while both the worker and his employer have a substantial role in prevention. To the extent that the employer does not receive adequate benefits from safety measures, his prevention expenditures will not fully reflect the total benefits of prevention. This situation, of course, parallels the case where a steel firm does not bear the costs of pollution and hence produces a socially undesirable amount of pollution.

Just as economic theory predicts that the amount of pollution may be optimized even with differential private and social costs, it also predicts that the amount of safety and health may be optimized under analogous circumstances. If workers accurately perceive the risks of accidents and disease and if there are negligible costs of bargaining with employers, an optimal safety level can be achieved. Under such circumstances the cost of taking risks would be reflected in the wage structure. That is, in order to attract workers to risky work the employer would have to pay a wage premium. The extra wages reflecting compensation for danger are the mechanism by which the firm is made to carry the burden of not preventing accidents and disease. Insofar as the employer devotes resources to prevention, the wage premium needed to attract workers will decrease. Thus, true social costs are made to be the employer's private costs. By preventing accidents for employees, an employer receives a benefit for himself—a reduction in his wage bill. This arrangement, based on a private exchange between employers and employees, would yield the optimal amount of safety and health because the relevant decision makers feel the full burden and rewards of both costs and benefits.

Are workers and employers likely to be fully aware of injury and prevention costs? It is difficult to answer this question. Many observers feel that workers do not accurately perceive the risks and cost of injury. The typical worker is often viewed as having the philosophy, "It will never happen to me." Although this view is intuitively no more appealing than the contrary view that the average worker is inappropriately fearful of his environment, neither view is based on compelling evidence.[6]

---

[6] Studies of the wage-premium issue include: R. Thaler and S. Rosen, "The Value of Saving a Life: Evidence from the Labor Market" (Paper presented at the National Bureau of Economic Research Conference, Washington, D.C., November 30, 1973); R. Smith, "The Feasibility of an 'Injury Tax' Approach to Occupational Safety," *Law and Contemporary Problems* (Summer-Autumn 1974), pp. 730-44; and J. Chelius, "The Control of Industrial Accidents: Economic Theory and Empirical Evidence," *Law and Contemporary Problems* (Summer-Autumn 1974), pp. 700-29.

As to the ease of bargaining and enforcing contracts, it is again difficult to make a judgment. Certainly bargaining between parties with an ongoing contractual relationship, such as employers and employees, is cheaper and easier than bargaining between a steel factory manager and a neighboring home owner. Unfortunately there is no solid empirical evidence to guide us on these issues. Even if we had direct evidence there would be no reliable standard by which to judge it. For example, how much information is necessary before an accurate system of risk-compensating wage premiums will develop? At what point do bargaining and enforcement mechanisms become too costly to facilitate health and safety agreements? There are no a priori standards by which to judge these matters. The need for empirical evidence is obviously great; however, we do not have firm answers to any of these critical questions. Whether private individual and group exchange can optimize safety and health remains an unanswered question, although the longstanding assumption by public policy makers is that it cannot. It is this unsupported assumption that has led to the conclusion that the government has a positive role to play in this area.

Even if it were determined that the private interactions of employees and employers do not yield an optimal amount of safety, it does not necessarily follow that government could improve the situation. Theoretical or practical misfunctionings in private markets should not be compared with a theoretical ideal of perfect government intervention, that is, socially optimal production by government fiat. The relevant comparison is between the practical realities of the marketplace and the practical realities of government regulation.

Who Causes Accidents?

One of the important factors that shapes policy is the actual source of industrial accidents. Who, or what, causes them? Various studies have found a startlingly wide range in the proportion of work accidents caused by employees (2 to 88 percent). Perhaps this is not so surprising given the lack of rigorous design in most of the studies.

The most thorough and credible analysis of accidents on the job appears to be a recent study sponsored by the state of Wisconsin.[7] The Wisconsin study found that approximately 45 percent of work injuries are due to careless behavior by workers, such as misuse of hand tools. An additional 30 percent are attributable to momentary

---

[7] Wisconsin State Department of Labor, Industry, and Human Relations, *Inspection Effectiveness Report* (1971).

physical hazards like open file drawers and wet floors. The remaining 25 percent of work injuries are caused by permanent physical factors like improperly guarded machines. The last category is the only one we might reasonably expect to reduce by the compulsory safety rules and inspection approach to regulation. Although there have been no formal studies, it would appear that the employee's role in disease prevention is not as critical as it is in accident prevention. The employee, of course, still has a role in disease prevention through careful use of the available prevention equipment, conscientious adherence to prescribed procedures, and monitoring of individual health.[8]

The employee's role in prevention is crucial because an effective policy must consider the underlying causes of accidents and diseases.[9] The current methods of regulation—both safety rules and workers' compensation—are geared toward the employer's role in prevention. Since many accidents and illnesses are not caused by the employer, the potential effectiveness of such regulation is limited. As an example of such policy ineffectiveness, consider the federal government's effort to make driving safer by mandating head rests on all new cars. There is no doubt that such head rests can help passengers avoid injuries from a crash. The National Safety Council, however, estimates that 80 percent of all drivers do not bother to adjust these head rests so that they will do any good. Similarly, in occupational safety regulation via controls on work environment, there will be little impact unless workers have incentives to act carefully.

Government officials have been reluctant to design public policies that recognize the employee's critical role in accident prevention. For example, in its concern about the impact of noise on workers' hearing, the government unhesitatingly requires expensive changes in the physical environment rather than less expensive worker-protection gear. A kind interpretation of the government's approach to prevention is the paternalistic one that workers must be protected from their own indiscretions. A cynic might argue that workers have far more votes than employers.

---

[8] As an example of the worker's role in disease prevention, there is anecdotal evidence that textile workers are reluctant to wear available face masks, which offer some protection from lung diseases. This reluctance is apparently due to the discomfort associated with the masks.

[9] Sam Peltzman, *Regulation of Automobile Safety* (Washington, D.C.: American Enterprise Institute, 1975), finds that the National Highway Safety Administration has been ineffective in reducing auto accidents for lack of recognition of their underlying causes.

The Goals of Public Policy

Although we have concentrated on the role of public policy in achieving an optimal quantity of accident and disease prevention, workers' compensation has an additional goal. This goal is to alleviate a worker's financial hardship resulting from an injury.[10] This objective is usually labeled income maintenance or income security. Although income maintenance is viewed by many as the sole purpose of workers' compensation, this is not a compelling foundation for such a policy. It makes little sense to have a separate and rather complicated system that distinguishes work injuries from nonwork injuries and other sources of poverty unless the system also serves the goal of encouraging an appropriate amount of safety and health.

There is, unfortunately, a conflict between the efficient prevention and the income-maintenance objectives of workers' compensation. The conflict is best illustrated by considering two extremes—one in which the income-maintenance goal is completely ignored and one in which workers suffer absolutely no penalty from an injury.

If all forms of insurance against financial loss due to injury were prohibited, the incentive for employees to avoid accidents would certainly be maximized. Employees would take extraordinary measures to avoid uninsured losses caused by injury. Some observers feel that the potential physical suffering of an injury already provides a maximum safety incentive, but there can be little doubt that financial incentives are also important. For example, avoiding personal injuries is an important motive in home fire prevention. However, the importance of this incentive should not distract us from the role played by the financial protection of fire insurance. If insurance were not available, most of us would surely take additional measures to protect our homes with smoke detectors, electrical wiring checkups, and decreased use of fireplaces, candles, and matches. Similarly, in a work setting a complete lack of insurance protection would surely eliminate some horseplay and reckless driving and increase the use of safety equipment like hardhats, goggles, and gloves.

---

[10] Some literature on workers' compensation further differentiates the system's goals. For example, the National Commission on State Workmen's Compensation Laws distinguished between the provision of income and medical care to injured workers. The notion of "income maintenance" in this volume is intended to encompass all forms of benefits to injured workers. Similarly, a distinction is sometimes made between encouragement of safety and the allocation of injury costs to the productive process. Any system that achieves the goal of "efficient prevention" as described in this volume would also allocate injury costs to the appropriate productive process.

On the other hand, if there were 100 percent protection against all losses due to accidents, including full compensation for lost salary, pain, and loss of leisure, a worker would tend to be indifferent to accident prevention. This policy extreme would satisfy the income-maintenance goal, but it would have a most undesirable effect on safety since workers would lose nothing from injury.

Certainly a generous insurance plan will not cause many people to take risks that they think will cause death or serious injury. However, such financial protection might induce people to take risks that involve the possibility of minor injuries. Unfortunately, these minor risks sometimes turn out to have very serious consequences. A worker might for convenience remove the guard from a machine because he "knows" the only risk is a bruised hand. However, it is just such actions that too often result in severed hands rather than bruises.

The extremes of no income protection and complete income protection illustrate the conflict between the prevention and the income-maintenance objectives of workers' compensation. As income-maintenance benefits increase, the cost of an accident to an employee decreases. Accordingly, his incentive to avoid an accident also decreases. Conversely, while low income-maintenance benefits give employees added incentive to avoid accidents, they do not satisfy the demand for income maintenance or provide any additional prevention incentives for employers. As a practical matter, low income-maintenance benefits might not even yield the extra prevention incentives for employees, since other forms of income maintenance, such as welfare benefits financed by general tax revenues, would likely be used to prevent an injured worker from suffering the full financial consequences of an injury. Our society does have a general income-maintenance goal, and any specific regulatory effort that ignores this objective will in all probability be displaced or supplemented by other programs.

The achievement of adequate income maintenance does not, of course, mean that workers must have full protection against every financial consequence of an injury. Some current workers' compensation laws, and proposals for reforming these laws, appear not to recognize the nature of the conflict between income maintenance and injury prevention and opt for virtually unrestrained fulfillment of the income-maintenance goal. A continuing theme of this volume is that while income maintenance and efficient prevention are both desirable goals, there unfortunately is a conflict between them. As a result, a compromise must be reached between them. It is a further theme of this analysis that the compromise embodied in the current system and suggested reforms overemphasizes income maintenance, while not being sufficiently sensitive to efficient accident and disease prevention.

The Reasons for Government Action

In this chapter we have reviewed the magnitude of work injuries, the causes of work injuries, and the possible difficulties of relying solely on either workers or employers to provide optimal safety and health. In one sense, these issues reflect the underlying nature of the problem and provide a basis for the analysis of specific policies to follow. There is, however, another perspective on occupational safety and health regulation. Although the data are not comprehensive, it is clear that occupational injury and death rates declined over most of the first sixty years of the twentieth century. During this period there was no substantial federal involvement in safety regulation. While all the states made some effort at regulation, in most it was minimal. Whatever the nature of the underlying work-injury problem and the potential inadequacies of private markets to ameliorate it, neither the public nor the government viewed this as an area that needed a new solution. This period of complacency ended in the mid-1960s, when work-injury rates began to drift upward, at least in the highly visible manufacturing sector. The increase in injury rates seems to have been at least the proximate cause of the greatly enlarged regulatory effort that began in 1970.[11] If we are fully to understand the potential impact of this new regulation, it is important to examine what caused the increase in work injuries during the 1960s.

For the post–World War II period, the pattern in manufacturing injury rates is illustrated in Figure 1. The generally downward slope before 1964 is followed by an increase through 1970—the latest year with comparable data. Starting in 1971, the definitions of injury rates were substantially changed in accordance with the mandate of the Occupational Safety and Health Act (OSHA), thus making the post-1970 data all but useless for the examination of long-run trends.

---

[11] Typical of the remarks about the need for new legislation is the following: "This 'grim current scene' . . . represents a worsening trend, for the fact is that the number of disabling injuries per million man hours worked is today 20 percent higher than in 1958. The knowledge that the industrial accident situation is deteriorating, rather than improving, underscores the need for action now" (Senator Harrison A. Williams [D-N.J.] in the report of the Committee on Labor and Public Welfare as reproduced in U.S. Congress, Senate, Committee on Labor and Public Welfare, *Legislative History of the Occupational Safety and Health Act of 1970* [92d Congress, 1971], p. 142).

Figure 1

THE INJURY FREQUENCY RATE, 1948-1970

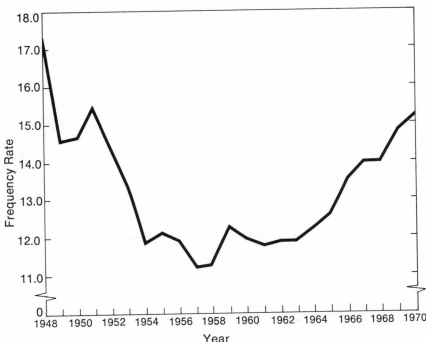

Note: The injury frequency rate is the number of disabling work injuries per million employee hours worked.

Source: U.S. Department of Labor, Bureau of Labor Statistics, *Handbook of Labor Statistics* (Washington, D.C., 1972).

The manufacturing work-injury data were collected by the United States Bureau of Labor Statistics. These data have frequently been criticized as inaccurate since data submissions were voluntary and quality control over the data was inadequate.[12] But these criticisms are irrelevant to the purpose at hand. Even if the data are biased, this will not interfere with an analysis of the trend as long as the bias is reasonably consistent over time.

In a 1972 article, Robert Smith documented the fact that variations in the level of business activity could explain a substantial portion of the year-to-year variations in injury rates.[13] Using the

---

12 An examination of the accuracy of pre-OSHA injury statistics is offered in Jerome Gordon et al., *Industrial Safety Statistics: A Re-examination* (New York: Praeger, 1971).
13 Robert S. Smith, "Intertemporal Changes in Work Injury Rates," *Proceedings of the Industrial Relations Research Association* (1973), pp. 167-74.

accession rate (the number of newly hired and rehired workers per 100 employees), I estimated the influence of the business cycle on injury rates. The injury rates used were from the manufacturing sector for the period 1948 through 1970.[14] I found that about 41 percent of the year-to-year injury-rate changes could be explained by this independent variable.[15] I then estimated the impact of an additional factor not considered by Smith—the changing age distribution of workers. It is well documented that younger workers have more work accidents (as well as nonwork accidents) than older workers. It is speculated in the literature on accidents that the higher injury rates for younger workers are due both to their inexperience and to their more careless behavior. Studies indicate that workers aged eighteen to thirty-five have higher injury rates than other age groups.[16] Because of this I used the percentage of workers eighteen to thirty-five as a proxy for the impact of the changing age composition of the labor force. The addition of an independent variable for worker age increased the power of the model to predict injury-rate changes from 41 percent of the variation to 53 percent.

To determine whether the increases in the period 1964 through 1970 were well explained by these factors, an additional analysis was undertaken. Using the relationship between changes in injury rates and the independent variable derived from the period 1948 through 1963, predictions for 1964–1970 were made. The relationships from 1948 through 1963 predicted injury rates for the subsequent period well within the range of error attributable to sampling variations. Thus, it is quite clear that no new problem had developed during this period. The factors that had been causing variations in injury rates were continuing their influence in a predictable manner. Apparently the continued upswing in the business cycle combined with an increasing proportion of younger workers was responsible for the increase in injury rates.

Although these results are statistically satisfying, it is important that they also be theoretically sound. Statistics can demonstrate correlation, not causation. A reasonable theory of causation is necessary. That an increase in the level of business activity would cause an increase in injury rates finds solid theoretical support. During an

---

[14] The injury rate used was the injury-frequency rate, which is defined as the number of disabling work injuries per million employee-hours of exposure. Work injuries include occupational diseases.

[15] Multiple regression was the statistical tool used in the analysis. Appendix A contains a more detailed description of the statistical procedures and results.

[16] Ernest McCormick and Joseph Tiffin, *Industrial Psychology* (London: George Allen and Unwin Ltd., 1975), pp. 524-26.

upswing, experienced employees work longer hours at a faster pace; fatigue and the pace are bound to take a toll in injuries. At the same time many new workers are being hired who will have a disproportionately high injury rate because of their inexperience and unfamiliarity with the hazards of their jobs. As already noted, a change in the number of younger workers can also be expected to cause a change in the number of injuries, since younger workers have less experience and tend to be more careless than older workers.

If the problem is, as analyzed, related to the business cycle and the age composition of the labor force, how likely is it that OSHA will ameliorate it? There is nothing in the compulsory-safety-rules approach of OSHA that will influence the business cycle or the age of workers. One could argue that compulsory safety rules are more necessary with a less careful labor force. But if carelessness is the ultimate cause, the rules are not responsive to the underlying cause and are not likely to be very successful. Similarly, there may be a greater need for income-maintenance aspects of workers' compensation to offset the higher injury rate, but there is nothing in this policy to promote safer work practices.

The problem should inevitably run its course as young workers from the post–World War II baby boom become older and more experienced. Just as inevitable will be the claim by government regulators that it was their wisdom and effort which led to the predestined reduction in injuries.

2

THE WORKERS' COMPENSATION SYSTEM

The History of Industrial Accident Liability Law

In order to understand fully the present workers' compensation system it is necessary to review both the history of that system and the tort system it replaced. Before the enactment of workers' compensation, damages arising from industrial accidents were assigned via a liability system based on fault, essentially the same system that is still used for most nonindustrial accidents. The party adjudged negligent in causing the accident was liable for the costs. In some states the definitions of negligence were statutory, whereas other states relied on the common law.

The pre-workers' compensation law of industrial-accident liability is best summarized by reference to the standards of conduct imposed on employers and employees.[1] It was the task of a jury to determine whether each party acted according to these standards. The basic duty of the employer was due care for employee safety. No negligence would be charged to the employer if he provided the safety precautions that a reasonably prudent man would take if he himself were in the employee's situation. The standard of due care, however, was far from absolute. A higher standard of employer caution was required in especially hazardous employment, such as railroading and mining, and where employees were young or inexperienced. As part of an employer's due care he was obligated to provide safe tools and equipment, although this did not include a duty to have the latest safety innovations. The custom of prudent men was the standard of safety required

---

[1] The following discussion is based largely on Lindley D. Clark, "The Legal Liability of Employers for Injuries to Their Employees in the United States," *Bulletin of the Bureau of Labor*, no. 74 (January 1908), pp. 1-120, and W. L. Prosser, *Law of Torts*, 4th ed. (St. Paul: West Publishing Co., 1971), pp. 525-40.

for tools and equipment. The employer was not considered negligent if an employee used tools for other than their intended purpose or if he used other than the customary procedure in performing a task. The employer was obligated to provide a sufficient number of qualified employees, and sufficient tools, to perform the work. In order to substantiate a charge of employer negligence on the basis that he had hired unqualified employees, the employer had to be shown to have had constructive or actual knowledge that the worker was unqualified.[2]

Employers also had responsibility for promulgating and enforcing reasonable rules for the safe conduct of business. The required standard was that following these rules with ordinary care would prevent reasonably foreseeable accidents. There was stronger obligation for enforcing the rules upon younger workers, who were unlikely to understand the risks associated with a particular job. Actual or implied knowledge of the rules by employees was necessary. Employers were required to give warnings about any dangers of which employees might excusably be ignorant.

Under the common law, an employer not meeting these standards of behavior would still not be considered negligent, and therefore liable for accident costs, if he could invoke one of three major defenses. These defenses were the negligence of fellow-servants (co-workers), the knowledgeable assumption of risk by employees, and contributory negligence by injured workers. According to the fellow-servant rule, an employer was not liable for the negligence of co-workers to each other unless a co-worker was acting as the employer's representative. The assumption-of-risk defense was that by agreeing to an employment contract, an employee was accepting any ordinary risks of that employment and any extraordinary risks that were known and accepted. The role of voluntary acceptance is emphasized by the fact that assumptions-of-risk did not apply to employees who were not immediately free to leave, such as convicts and seamen. Contributory negligence was deemed to have occurred if the injured worker could have avoided the consequences of the employer's negligence by the exercise of ordinary care.

These common law defenses could be viewed as an effort to achieve an efficient mix of accident prevention by employers and employees. Richard Posner offers such an interpretation:

> The fellow-servant rule . . . provides, in principle at least, a
> powerful instrument for industrial safety when combined

---

[2] *Constructive knowledge* in this context means that the circumstances imply the employer had such knowledge, without regard to any evidence that he actually had the knowledge.

with the rule making the employer liable for injuries inflicted on an employee through the negligence of a fellow employee if the employer was on notice of the fellow employee's habitual neglect or incompetence. The effect of the two rules [the fellow-servant rule plus the duty to provide qualified coworkers] is to give employees a strong incentive to report careless fellow workers to their supervisors.[3] /

Posner interprets the assumption-of-risk rule as a method of enabling workers with a positive taste for risk to market that taste. He sees contributory negligence as a rule that encourages the party who can most cheaply prevent an accident to take appropriate precautions. This incentive is present because the failure of such a person to prevent an accident would make him liable even if another person could have prevented the accident but only at a higher cost.

To evaluate the effectiveness of this legal environment in fostering industrial safety, the number of accidents actually compensated must be considered, just as one must evaluate the conviction rate as well as penalties in studying criminal behavior. Reports from the period indicate that from 6 to 30 percent of industrial accidents were compensated by employers.[4] This seemingly low compensation rate could be consistent with the provision of efficient incentives. If it were the more serious injuries that were compensated, the incentives might still be the correct ones for achieving an efficient allocation of prevention resources. Since there are administrative costs in assigning and dispensing compensation, the benefits of foregoing compensation for minor injuries might be outweighed by the costs. This is analogous to the situation where administrative costs preclude the development of a market for a specific good or service. Although the absence of an explicit market is often cited as a demonstration of inefficiency, this may only indicate that the costs of administering the market are being economized. For example, there frequently is no explicit market in shopping center parking spaces. The costs of charging individual prices for each space are high enough that it becomes efficient to combine the price of such space with the price of the products purchased at the shopping center. Certainly, the absence of an explicit market in parking spaces is not an indication of inefficient allocation of resources. Similarly, the absence of compensation for minor injuries could be an indication of efficiency. Even with such "transaction costs," the efficient solution would not require employers to pay the costs of all

---

[3] Richard Posner, "A Theory of Negligence," *The Journal of Legal Studies*, vol. 1, no. 1 (1972), p. 44.

[4] Prosser, *Law of Torts*, p. 530.

accidents, since employees are frequently at fault. The ambiguity of the situation emphasizes the need for empirical evidence.

Many states passed statutory modifications of the common law. These statutes, known as employer's liability laws, frequently modified or completely abolished the fellow-servant rule and other employer defenses. The laws also frequently made an employer's failure to comply with government safety codes a basis for negligence. Although the definitions of negligent behavior were changed by these laws, the essence of the negligence system was preserved. Liability for accident costs was still based on a determination of which party was at fault.

Beginning in 1911, the states started to enact workmen's compensation laws which have subsequently become known as workers' compensation laws. Under workers' compensation, an employer is obligated to pay employees or their heirs a governmentally determined benefit, frequently less than the full accident costs, regardless of the cause of the work injury. In exchange for immunity from employee damage suits for the full costs of accidents, the employer is required to pay a portion of accident costs for all work injuries. Workers' compensation is essentially a system of compulsory insurance where benefit levels are established by the state government and premiums are paid by the employer. This arrangement represents the first example of what later became known as no-fault insurance systems.

The Contemporary System

An understanding of the contemporary workers' compensation system requires consideration of the following issues: (1) the coverage of workers, (2) the definition of compensable injuries and diseases, (3) the structure and amount of benefits, (4) the insurance arrangements that guarantee these benefits, (5) the administration of the system, and (6) the relationship between workers' compensation benefits and other income-security programs.[5]

Worker Coverage. In 1974, approximately 87 percent of the United States labor force was covered by the provisions of the various workers' compensation laws. Only railroad workers and seamen are universally excluded from the laws. These workers are subject to the Federal Employer's Liability Act, which gives them the right to sue employers for damages in a tort proceeding. Under this system, the accused employers cannot use the common law defenses of assumption of risk or fellow-servant negligence. The defense of contributory

[5] An extensive summary of the workers' compensation system may be found in: National Commission on State Workmen's Compensation Laws, *Compendium on Workmen's Compensation* (Washington, D.C., 1973). Much of the material for this section is based on this volume.

negligence is changed to comparative negligence so that a negligent worker's claim for damages is reduced in proportion to his own negligence rather than being completely eliminated. Under the traditional contributory negligence defense, an employer would be absolved of all responsibility for accident costs if he could demonstrate that the injured worker's failure to exercise reasonable care contributed to the accident. Under comparative negligence, if a worker's negligence contributed 10 percent to an accident, the damage award for the injury would be discounted by 10 percent. Efforts to provide workers' compensation coverage to railroad workers and seamen have been resisted by their unions. They feel they are better off under the modified tort system, which provides a larger percentage of actual damages than does workers' compensation when the employer is proven to have been negligent.

Other workers may not be covered by workers' compensation because the law in their state is elective. When employers were made liable for employee accident costs regardless of actual fault, early court decisions declared that this responsibility deprived them of property without due process of law. To counteract this contention, many early workers' compensation statutes were elective for the employer. Under such a law an employer can choose not to have his employees covered. However, he is then subject to tort action by his employees. Under most elective laws an employer who rejects coverage forfeits the use of the common law defenses of assumed risk of employment, negligence of fellow-servants, and contributory negligence by the injured worker. Compulsory coverage has been declared constitutional, but a few states still maintain elective laws. If an employer is not subject to either an elective or compulsory workers' compensation law, in most jurisdictions he may voluntarily bring himself under the provisions of the law. As of July 1, 1975, workers' compensation was generally compulsory for private employers in forty-six of the fifty-one jurisdictions (fifty states plus the District of Columbia), although ten states permit some employees to waive their coverage.[6]

Further, many states exempt specific occupations from coverage. Twenty states fully cover farmworkers under their laws, while only four states fully cover household and casual workers. State and local government employees are also exempted in seven states. Most states

---

[6] Unless otherwise noted, the current status of laws is defined as of July 1, 1975. The source for the July 1, 1975 provisions of the laws is Ad Hoc Committee to Consider State Compliance with Workers' Compensation Recommended Standards, *Substantial Compliance of State Laws with Workers' Compensation Recommended Standards* (unpublished manuscript, available from John F. Binton, University of Chicago, March 1976).

also exclude some other classes of employees such as professional athletes, employees of charitable organizations, newscarriers, or hazardous or nonhazardous jobs in general. In most cases, the rationale for exemption is the administrative difficulty of covering such workers or the absence of an employer engaged in commercial business. Administrative difficulty is also the reason some states exempt employers who have a small number of employees.

Injury Coverage. Although the concept of a work injury is, in the abstract, straightforward, in practice substantial litigation has been required to specify its exact meaning. Even if the employee is covered by workers' compensation, an injury he receives must meet certain conditions to be compensable by the employer or by his insurance company. In general, the test for compensability is that an employee must have received (1) a personal injury (2) as the result of an accident (3) which arose out of and (4) in the course of employment. Although most of the states have adopted these concepts, the language and interpretation of specific statutes varies.

Personal injury is usually defined broadly so as to include mental disabilities, nervous disorders, infections, and diseases as well as physical damage to the body. The basic conditions for an injury to be considered accidental are that it be the result of something unexpected and that it be traceable to some definite time, place, occasion, or cause. In most states the injury need not be the result of unusual work or exertion. For example, a heart attack or back injury suffered as a result of ordinary exertion is typically compensable.

The concept of "arising out of employment" has been the subject of much litigation and is interpreted in a variety of ways. It is universally accepted that an injury is compensable if it was the result of a risk directly associated with employment. If an injury results from a distinctly personal risk, that is, a peril affecting all people, it is generally not compensable. Controversies develop over less identifiable risks that are a combination of employment and personal risks. In an effort to distinguish employment risks from the general risks of life, courts have set various criteria. For example, consider an employee struck by lightning while on the job. In some jurisdictions such an injury would be compensable only if the job had increased his probability of being struck by lightning. Other jurisdictions use a positional risk test that would imply compensation if the worker's employment had caused him to be in danger where and when he was at the time of the accident. If an injury is related to a personal condition that existed before employment, such as a weak back, the usual rule is that the injury is compensable if the employment contributed to aggravation, weakening, or acceleration of the preexisting condition. For example, an ordinarily noncompensable heart attack would be compensated if, because of his job, the victim were positioned to fall off a ladder because of the attack.

Complications to a compensable injury are also covered by workers' compensation unless they result from the intentional acts of the injured worker. Thus an injury received on the way to a doctor's office to obtain care for a compensable injury is covered. Similarly the results of incorrect treatment by an independent physician attending a covered injury are also the employer's responsibility. Of course if the treatment is negligent the doctor may also be held liable in a separate legal action. Complications that result from an employee's intentional acts such as refusing reasonable medical treatment are not covered by workers' compensation.

The "course of employment" concept relates to the time, place, and activity when the injury occurred. The standards for compensability vary depending on the type of employee. Workers who normally are in a fixed facility for the work day are termed inside employees. Outside workers are those like traveling salesmen or truck drivers. A third category consisting of those who live on the employer's premises or who are on twenty-four-hour call is also distinguished. The typical inside employee is considered to be in the course of his employment from the moment he enters the employer's premises until he leaves. This includes company parking lots, stairways, and elevators. Resting and reasonable horseplay as well as direct work are considered to take place in the course of employment. The criteria for outside workers are broader and include virtually all the time and activities between leaving and returning home. The guidelines for on-premises or on-call workers are varied, but in general a very broad range of these workers' activities are considered to be employment related.

Compensability has proven to be an especially difficult issue in regard to occupational diseases. For many years a common administrative device was to cover only those occupational diseases specifically listed in the statute. This is known as schedule coverage. Almost all states (forty-seven out of fifty-one jurisdictions) currently provide full coverage for all occupational diseases. The primary administrative problem with such diseases appears to be the long period of exposure necessary for contraction and the obscure nature of the causes of many diseases. As an example of the difficulties, consider a miner who has black-lung disease after thirty years in various mines. There is no straightforward manner in which to determine the employer responsible for the disability payments.

Benefits. Workers' compensation provides payments in five benefit categories: (1) medical expenses only, (2) temporary total disability, (3) permanent partial disability, (4) permanent total disability, and (5) death. About 80 percent of work injuries require only medical care with no income-replacement benefits. Most states (forty-five of fifty-one jurisdictions) place no restrictions on either the amount or duration of medical-service benefits. In some states, the injured employee may choose his own doctor, while in other states the choice of a doctor is the employer's. Medical-care benefits constitute over one-third of all workers' compensation benefits paid. In 1974, medical benefits totaled more than $1.7 billion.

If an injured employee is unable to work but has the prospect of returning to employment after either full or partial recovery, he is eligible for temporary total benefits after a waiting period of two to seven days. The waiting period is analogous to the deductible provision in most medical and automobile insurance policies. Having the employee responsible for the most minor of income losses is designed to minimize administrative costs and discourage unnecessary absence from work. If the disability lasts beyond a specified time ranging from five to forty-nine days, the worker is retroactively eligible for the benefits covering the waiting period. Over 70 percent of all cases that require income-replacement benefits are in the temporary category. Temporary total benefits are based on a percentage of the injured worker's gross wages. The amount of wages replaced varies from 60 to 90 percent with 66⅔ percent the amount most frequently used. Benefits in all jurisdictions are subject to a weekly maximum which varies substantially among states. Some states also limit the duration of the benefits, the limits running from 208 to 600 weeks. Total benefit limits are also used in some states. These range from $20,000 to $74,500.

If a worker is permanently disabled but still capable of some kind of regular work, he is eligible for permanent partial benefits. The determination of the extent of partial disability is one of the most controversial administrative aspects of workers' compensation. Such cases account for more than 60 percent of the nonmedical benefits paid, although they represent only slightly more than 25 percent of the compensable injuries. For administrative convenience, many such injuries are compensated according to an established schedule of benefits. Injuries paid according to a schedule are typically the most easily defined, such as the loss of an arm, hand, eyesight, or hearing.

24

The structure of benefits available for scheduled injuries is basically the same as for temporary total-disability benefits. An exception is that the duration of benefits is usually fixed by the schedule rather than being dependent on the actual time out of work. If a permanent partial injury is not on the schedule, the benefits are set by a hearing officer appointed by the state workers' compensation agency. Benefits are based on a combination of financial loss and physical impairment with the relative importance of each factor varying in different states. Benefits are stated in terms of a percentage of wages subject to weekly and total maximums.

About 0.1 percent of all cases are permanent injuries that are considered totally disabling. The standards for total disability differ among the states. They may be based on inability to perform available work or on major physical impairments like blindness or the loss of two limbs. In the event of death, benefits are usually paid to the spouse until death or remarriage and to children until they come of age. The benefits are for a portion of wages, typically 66⅔ percent, with weekly benefits subject to a maximum. The total amount of benefits is also limited in a few jurisdictions.

Insurance Arrangements. In most states workers' compensation laws require firms to insure against potential financial liabilities to injured workers. The insurance may be provided by a private insurance company, a state-operated insurance fund, or a self-insurance plan. While a few states require employers to insure with a governmental insurance fund, most states either do not have a state fund or have one that operates in competition with private insurance companies and self-insurance.

The most significant aspect of the insurance arrangements is the manner of assessing premium charges. If workers' compensation is to contribute to efficient accident prevention, the premiums charged to a firm must reflect its prevention efforts. The ideal premium arrangement is one in which premiums are discounted by the costs of the accidents prevented. Thus if an employer spent $100 to prevent a $150 accident, it would be desirable for his insurance premium to be reduced by the $150 expense that has been avoided.

This finely tuned adjustment is approached only when the firm acts as its own insurer. In this situation, any costs saved by preventing an accident benefit the firm. Thus self-insurance maximizes the firm's incentive for providing safe working conditions. For those firms which meet their insurance obligations through private insurance companies, the relationship between premiums and benefits is never as direct. However, the sensitivity of insurance prices to company experience is greater as firm size increases. If the firm buying insurance from a private insurer or from a state fund is sufficiently large to provide a statistically reliable accident experience, it is eligible for reductions in the price of insurance based on the firm's injury experience. Firms not large enough to qualify for premiums based on their own experience are charged on the basis of the industrial classification of their firm. For such firms, workers' compensation does not contribute to the incentive to prevent accidents. This is not to say that small employers have no incentive to prevent accidents. Actual injury frequencies among small employers are significantly less than those of intermediate size firms.

Approximately one-fourth of the employers carrying workers' compensation insurance are eligible for experience-based pricing (merit rating). These firms are, of course, the larger employers and account for about 85 percent of the dollar volume of premiums. Firms which self-insure account for about 14 percent of benefits paid. The formula used to set premiums for experience-rated firms involves a comparison between their specific experience and the average of all firms in their industrial classification.

Administration. One of the original goals of workers' compensation was the elimination of lengthy and costly legal proceedings, but the system still requires substantial administrative effort. The first step in processing a worker's compensation claim is filing an injury report with the state agency administering the system. The insurance company, or the employer in the case of self-insurance, is responsible for the initial processing. Usually the insurance company looks into the injury and the circumstances surrounding it and reaches an agreement with the employee. In such cases the state agency's involvement is not extensive. Some states inform injured employees of their rights or even approve settlements. In most states, however, the agencies' role in uncontested cases is passive, involving only such functions as gathering injury statistics and checking for duplicate claims. Estimates of the number of uncontested cases vary from 70 to 90 percent.

If a worker is not satisfied with the settlement offered or if the employer has denied liability, the worker may file a claim with the state agency. Typically, the first stage of this quasi-judicial process is an informal conference at which an agency representative attempts to find a settlement or at least arrive at a mutually acceptable version of the facts surrounding the injury. If the case is not settled through these proceedings, a formal hearing is conducted by a state hearing

26

officer. The degree of formality at such hearings varies substantially among the states. The hearing officer's decision settles the case unless either party chooses to appeal to the administrative review body of the agency, usually the workers' compensation commissioners or an independent review board. If either party is still not satisfied, the case may be appealed to a state court.

Relationship to Other Remedies. Although workers' compensation is by far the most significant remedy for injured employees, other programs may affect them. Tort actions, based on alleged negligence, may be available to the injured worker, as well as private and public insurance plans.

A basic principle of workers' compensation is that the employer provides a guaranteed payment for injuries, even when they are not his fault, in exchange for limitations on the extent of his financial liability. There are, however, a few circumstances under which an allegedly negligent employer can be sued for the full value of the damages from a work injury. If an employer fails to cover his employees by workers' compensation, either through lawful election not to cover or failure to comply with the law, he is liable to a tort action by an injured worker for full damages. For damages to be assessed the employer must be proven to have been negligent. However, in defending the suit, he may not use the common law defenses of contributory negligence by the employee, the negligence of fellow-workers, or the assumption of risk by the injured worker. In some jurisdictions, an employee may sue for damages beyond workers' compensation benefits, even when he is covered by the program, if the employer's actions are considered willful misconduct, such as assault, or willful failure to provide safety devices.

An injured worker may also bring suit against a negligent party other than the employer. Common examples of this include actions against the producer of defective work machinery or the landlord of a hazardous building. Under certain limited circumstances such third parties may, in turn, seek recovery from the employer, if his negligence also contributed to the injury. In the past, many states required the injured employee to elect either negligence litigation or workers' compensation, but not both. Today every state except one allows actions in both systems.

The most widespread insurance program for injured workers other than workers' compensation is social security. The social security program provides benefits to totally disabled workers, retired workers, and the survivors of deceased workers. These benefits sometimes overlap with those received under workers' compensation, although the payments from social security are reduced if the disabled person is also receiving workers' compensation. Disability benefits are paid under both social security and workers' compensation in about 1 percent of the new workers' compensation cases. However, since these cases represent long term disabilities, the proportion of workers receiving both benefits at any time is greater than 1 percent.

Other social insurance programs that overlap slightly with workers' compensation are unemployment insurance, welfare for the permanently and totally disabled, Medicaid, and veterans' pensions for disabilities not connected with military service. California, Hawaii, New Jersey, New York, and Rhode Island have compulsory insurance programs covering workers temporarily disabled by illness or non-occupational injuries. These programs cover disabilities not included under workers' compensation.

A myriad of private programs also cover the financial losses of occupational injuries. The most common is life insurance. About 70 percent of all employees are covered by group life insurance policies, and many workers, of course, have individual policies. About 70 percent of all workers also have medical insurance. Counting individual and company plans, over three-fourths of the civilian population have some insurance protection against the costs of health care. Also popular, although covering less than half the work force, are pension plans with provisions for early retirement based on disability. If sick leave is included, a majority of workers have some sort of temporary disability insurance. Plans that provide only sick leave, however, would not fully cover an extended disability. The trend for all of these private voluntary insurance plans is one of substantial growth. Less expensive group rates and tax-free premiums make the plans especially attractive as company fringe benefits.

Conclusions

The workers' compensation system has been in use in the United States for over sixty-five years. It developed because of dissatisfaction with a liability system that relied solely on determinations of negligent behavior. Workers' compensation has yielded well-defined and reasonably certain standards of what constitutes a compensable work-related injury.

Before we judge whether this system is satisfactory or in need of reform it is important to consider the alternatives. The next chapter will review the theoretical and empirical issues raised by workers' compensation and other policies for regulating industrial safety.

3

ALTERNATIVE POLICIES FOR REGULATING INDUSTRIAL SAFETY

Although the goal of this volume is the evaluation of workers' compensation, it is useful to consider other alternatives for exercising control over the causes and consequences of work injuries. A knowledge of these alternatives will help us to understand the strengths and weaknesses of workers' compensation and other policies, and thus give us a broader perspective for making a summary evaluation of occupational safety and health regulation and the appropriate role of workers' compensation.

As we have seen, the goals of public policy toward industrial safety—income security for afflicted workers and efficient prevention of accidents and diseases—tend to conflict with one another. In theory, if we knew the relative values people placed on each, we could fashion a compromise. But individual preferences differ widely and cannot be evaluated with precision. We must therefore conduct our analysis with the foreknowledge that progress toward one goal probably cannot be made without hindering progress toward the other.

Other problems also arise. Any public policy that requires mandatory compliance has inherent costs not present in voluntary arrangements, both in dollars and in limitations on individual freedom. In relying on centrally dictated policy, compulsory insurance or compulsory safety rules may possibly serve the cause of optimal risk and security, but only with restraints on our freedom of action. Some contend that the costs of constrained freedom are no different from other safety costs and should simply be included in the cost/benefit calculus that yields the optimal policy. This may be unarguable as a theoretical issue, but in practice it seems impossible to compute such costs in a manner amenable to formal analysis. This is, of course, a problem with any "commodity" that is not traded in the marketplace.

Many different values are placed on such freedom. Some may value it highly; others may consider it unimportant in the context of regulating safety and health. Many argue that freedom from financial hardships, as manifested in the income-security goal, is the only freedom relevant to government safety policy. Because of the wide range of values individuals place on freedom, we will concentrate on the more concrete costs and benefits relating to safety and health. The impact of alternative government measures on personal choice will nonetheless be occasionally considered.

Alternative Policies in the Abstract

It is useful to consider each of the alternative public policies toward safety in isolation even if they are mixed in practice. Initially each system will be described as if there were no practical complications, then discussed as it would tend to operate amid the frictions of the real world.

The prototype policies toward safety are: (1) employee liability for accident costs, (2) employer liability for accident costs, (3) shared employee and employer liability for accident costs, (4) liability for accident costs based on which party is at fault, (5) government safety rules enforced by inspectors and fines, and (6) government income security financed by general tax revenues.

Employee Liability. If the control of industrial injuries were left to private markets, with workers bearing all of their accident costs and having no remedy for employer negligence, competitive labor markets with informed workers would yield higher wages to workers in hazardous jobs. The extra wage would be equal to what the workers adjudged to be the cost of the extra hazards of their jobs. Under such a system, two jobs differing only in hazards would be compensated at wage rates varying only by the value placed on that difference. If the wage rates differed by more than this, workers would shift to the higher paying job until the rates net of the hazardous-work premium were equalized. Similarly, if the rates differed by less than the value placed on risks, workers would shift away from the more hazardous jobs.

Under such an unfettered market system, an employer has a choice of how to deal with the risks faced by his employees. He can opt to do nothing about the risks and pay his employees a hazardous-work premium, or he can reduce the risks and pay his employees commensurately less. The risks can, of course, be reduced only by an expenditure of resources. To maximize profits, the employer will choose the combination of hazardous-work payments and accident-prevention expenditures that minimizes his combined labor and accident-prevention costs. The optimal combination of wage premiums and risk reduction expenditures will be determined by their relative prices. The rational employer will therefore devote resources to accident prevention as long as the expected marginal cost is less than the marginal return. His return would include a decrease in such direct accident costs as damaged machinery and lost production time as well as a lower hazardous-work premium. The resulting arrangement can be considered economically efficient to the individuals involved and to society because, on average, injuries will be prevented whenever the expected costs of the injury are greater than the expected costs of prevention.

Income security under this arrangement is up to the worker or his employer. Many employers would find it in their interest to provide income security for disabled workers under such a system,[1] just as many now find it advantageous to supplement legally required income security for disabled workers.

Employer Liability. If private markets were allowed to function but with the constraint of employer liability for all accident costs, the system would operate differently but would yield the same allocation of resources as an unfettered market system. The government would establish accident prices equal to the full cost of accidents to employees. Employers would then pay injured employees benefits equal to the government-mandated accident price. The employer would have what is termed automatic or strict liability (in the previous system the employee was strictly liable). Under a system of strict employer liability, the market would no longer yield a wage premium for hazardous work because the workers' expected injury costs, including discomfort due to the risk of accident, would be zero. Workers would be reimbursed for all of their costs in the form of postinjury compen-

---

[1] A review of major collective-bargaining agreements indicates that in 1971, 52 percent of all covered workers had greater protection from loss-of-income due to disability than is required by law. See James R. Chelius and Carl J. Schramm, "Decisions for Safety: A Model of the Firm," *Proceedings of the American Institute for Decision Sciences* (Atlanta: American Institute for Decision Sciences, 1974), pp. 185-87.

sation. As under the unfettered market system, the employer would take any prevention measures that return more than they cost. The employer will continue these expenditures until their expected marginal return is equal to their expected marginal cost.

The primary efficiency goal is to assure prevention when it costs less than the injury. Several prevention techniques are frequently available, many of which meet the standard of costing less than the injury. In this situation a desirable system has incentives which encourage the least costly prevention method. It is useful to see how liability systems operate in a situation where there are multiple prevention techniques. If a given type of accident can be prevented either with an investment in machinery or with a less costly investment in careful behavior by the workers, it would be efficient for the workers to prevent this type of accident. This efficient result will occur independently of which party has liability, if there are no costs to bargaining between employers and employees. If workers are liable for accident costs, they will prevent the accident. If the employer is liable, he can induce the employees to prevent this type of accident by paying them some part of the difference between the cost of machinery and the cost of careful behavior to the employee. Similarly, if the employer is most efficient at a particular aspect of prevention, he will undertake it under either employer or employee liability. If protective headgear is useful for accident prevention and it is less expensive when purchased by the employer, he will provide this equipment even under a system of employee liability. This occurs because it is the least costly method of avoiding accident costs. If employees purchased the headgear, the employer would have to pay indirectly for them in the form of higher wages that compensate employees for their purchase. Since the employer would save money by paying for the headgear directly rather than indirectly, the employer interested in maximizing profits would purchase the headgear even under employee liability.

The costs and returns of accident prevention are the same under both employee and employer liability systems. The only difference is in the form of the benefits. Under employee liability, prevention efforts will reduce the wage premium; under employer liability the return is a reduction in postinjury costs borne by the employer. Since the pattern of employee and employer prevention is the same, the allocation of resources is identical under either arrangement. The only real difference between the systems is that income security is mandatory under employer liability and voluntary under employee liability.

Shared Liability. One variation of the employer liability system requires the employer to provide postinjury payments to workers which are less than 100 percent of the employee's accident costs. This is actually a shared liability system because the employee must bear all accident costs not assigned to the employer. The present workers' compensation system essentially takes this form. Under shared liability the benefits of prevention for the employer would be manifested as a combination of lower hazardous-work premiums and lower postinjury costs. This occurs because the market would generate wage premiums reflecting the employee's accident costs not guaranteed by the firm. In total, the costs and benefits of accident prevention remain the same as under unilateral liability. Income security under this system would be mandatory for the employer's share of accident costs and voluntary for the employee's share.

The distribution of income does not vary under any of these systems. The worker is paid for the risks he takes in either wage premiums, postinjury compensation, or both. The firm's net outlays are also the same, with only the form of payment varying.

Liability Based on Fault. Under a fault system, an injured employee may sue his employer for damages. If the employer has not taken proper measures to prevent accidents, he will be liable for the full cost of the injury. Because the visible mechanics of court actions take place after a particular act, it is often overlooked that the possibility of court action would be a strong incentive for employers to promote safety. Such incentives take the form of legal precedents which provide a set of rules which the parties must obey if they are to avoid liability for damages. With an established body of common law, the probability of either employee or employer being liable for accident costs is determinable, although not necessarily with a high degree of confidence. If either party is considered negligent at law when he fails to undertake accident prevention measures that cost less than the injury costs, these legal rules will be economically efficient. As Posner notes, the negligence standard formulated by Judge Learned Hand takes this form. Hand's notion was that

> the judge (or jury) should attempt to measure three things in ascertaining negligence: the magnitude of the loss if an accident occurs; the probability of the accident's occurring; and the burden [cost] of taking precautions to prevent it. If the product of the first two terms, the expected benefit,

exceeds the burden of precautions, the failure to take those precautions is negligence.[2]

If an employee does not expect his full accident costs to be covered by court judgments against the employer, he will require a wage premium to equalize his remuneration with less risky opportunities. If the standards of safe behavior are changed so that the probability of the employer's paying injury costs changes, the wage premium will adjust to reflect this difference. For example, assume that under a fault system with a fellow-servant exemption for employer liability,[3] an employee perceives there is a 50 percent chance that he must bear all accident costs. If the fellow-servant rule is voided, thereby increasing the probability of employer liability, the accident cost burden to the employee is decreased, leading to a reduction in the wage premium required to attract employees.

The added costs of court liability determination may appear burdensome in that legal fees are usually a significant percentage of the total award.[4] The benefits of legal proceedings, however, *may* outweigh their costs. This could occur if the incentives created by

---

[2] Richard Posner, "A Theory of Negligence," p. 32. The negligence standard formulated by Judge Learned Hand is a derivation from two separate opinions. In the first, Conway v. O'Brian, 111 F.2d 611, 612 (2d Cir. 1940), Judge Hand wrote: "The degree of care demanded of a person . . . is the resultant of three factors: the likelihood that his conduct will injure others, taken with the seriousness of the injury if it happens, and balanced against the interest which he must sacrifice to avoid the risk." Judge Hand supplemented his original formulation in his opinion for the court in United States v. Carroll Towing Co., 159 F.2d 169, 173 (2d Cir. 1947), when he suggested that: "the owner's duty, as in other similar situations, to provide against resulting injuries is a function of three variables: (1) the probability that she [a barge] will break away; (2) the gravity of the resulting injury, if she does; (3) the burden of adequate precautions. Possibly it serves to bring this notion into relief to state it in algebraic terms: if the probability be called P; the injury, L; and the burden, B; liability depends upon whether B is less than L multiplied by P; that is, whether $B < PL$."

[3] The fellow-servant rule is that an employer is not liable for employee injuries which are caused by fellow employees.

[4] The presence of a seemingly burdensome cost is not necessarily a reliable measure of the efficiency of a system. Lee Benham, "The Effect of Advertising on the Price of Eyeglasses," *Journal of Law and Economics*, vol. 15, no. 2 (1972), pp. 337-52. This article examines the price of comparable eyeglasses in states which prohibited advertising and in states which allowed advertising. Even though advertising was found to be a substantial percentage of price in the states which allowed advertising, the total price of eyeglasses was significantly lower in advertising states. Benham ascribes this phenomenon to the fact that advertising provides information which, in turn, yields a more competitive and efficient market. Analogously, the presence of significant court costs does not necessarily mean that a tort system is inefficient. Like advertising, the benefits of legal proceedings may greatly outweigh their costs and be a necessary part of an efficient system.

such a system were more accurate and precise than those present under alternative systems. Furthermore, under relatively stable common law rules, large fees are not incurred frequently since cases go to court only when there are conflicting views as to the applicability of the negligence rules. Each party can usually foresee the outcome of a trial and is therefore often willing to settle out of court.[5]

Guaranteed income security is not inherent in the negligence system since payments are provided only if the employer is negligent. Of course, as under any other system that requires the employee to face the risk of disability, many employers will find it advantageous voluntarily to guarantee such support.

Government Safety Rules. Another possible regulatory mechanism for promoting industrial safety is government fiat, that is, the prohibition of workplace conditions and worker behavior known to be unsafe. If such a system is to be efficient, the government agency with jurisdiction must be: (1) aware of the costs of injuries to specific employees and employers, (2) aware of the efficient methods of preventing risk in individual workplaces, and (3) able to enforce efficiently rules that take such individual differences into account. Under these conditions, direct government intervention would yield the same result as the other control arrangements. A potential weakness of this type of control is that the government has no efficient way to be informed about conditions in individual workplaces. The more inspectors it maintains, the better informed it will be, but the greater the cost. Other control mechanisms such as strict and fault liability systems avoid this cost by requiring efficient injury prevention in general terms but leaving it to the participants who already know their workplace problems to work out the specific prevention methods which are most appropriate.

Guaranteed income security plays no part in the government fiat approach to safety and health. With each system working perfectly, the expected distribution of income under a fiat or tort system would be the same as under the unfettered market or government price incentives. In each case the employer would bear the burden of both injury prevention and the cost of employees' injuries. Similarly, the employee is reimbursed for the expected value of his accident costs under each system, although the form of compensation depends upon the control system.

---

[5] John Gould, "The Economics of Legal Conflicts," *Journal of Legal Studies*, vol. 2, no. 2 (1973), pp. 279–300.

Government Income Security. A final regulatory mechanism to consider is that of an income-security system financed by a tax on the employer's payroll. This contrasts with the workers' compensation system, which in many respects operates as an income-security system financed by a "tax" on injuries. Since a payroll tax does not vary with the number of injuries suffered, an employer will not receive the full benefit of injury-prevention expenditures. Under this arrangement, therefore, we can expect employers to spend relatively less on injury avoidance than under other systems. Similarly, we can expect workers to be less careful since they suffer no financial loss from accidents. The employee's accident costs are met by the government income-security program, so no wage premiums for hazardous work will develop, thus further reducing the employer's incentive to alleviate risk. The number, severity, and cost of accidents will therefore be greater in this system.

The income-security goal is met in full under such a system. If the benefits available to injured workers were less than the full cost of accidents, some wage premium for hazardous work would develop. The premium would depend on the portion of the accident costs paid by the income-security program. Partial income security would give employees a limited incentive to exercise more care insofar as they thought that an accident would not be fully compensated by higher wages.

Comparison of the Alternatives

If each system worked smoothly, the policy issues of safety and health would be straightforward. As long as the liability for accident costs is assigned either to the employer or to the employee, the result will be optimal safety and health. Perfectly designed government safety rules tailored to each establishment and its work force would yield the same result. As long as people engage in optimizing behavior, it makes no difference which form the rewards and costs take. The only policy that can distort this result is to assign liability to a third party, such as the government, with no incentive to prevent injury or to rehabilitate the injured. A government income-security system financed by a payroll tax instead of being based on injuries would fail to produce optimal safety. Since several systems yield the same level of safety and health, the choice of optimal policy can then be based on our desire for income security.

Although the largely theoretical discussions above are useful for understanding the potential workings of each system, they do not reflect the real world. No system operates so smoothly. Therefore, we are faced with the dilemma of which policy works best in practice. Once we acknowledge that the alternatives do not work perfectly, we cannot be certain of the optimal policy. The best policy mix depends not on the theoretical efficiency of the alternatives but on the degree to which practical complications are likely to keep policies from being efficient. These complications cannot be evaluated strictly on the basis of theory, so we need evidence about the actual working of each alternative. Before we review this evidence, let us consider the potential problems inherent in each system.

Information. If unfettered private markets are to yield an optimal level of safety and health, a set of reasonably accurate wage premiums reflecting risks must develop. These premiums are known as compensating differentials; they compensate the worker for bearing risks. If wage differentials are to reflect degrees of risk accurately, information about the riskiness of alternative jobs must be available. It is often claimed that employees consistently underestimate the probability and costs of accidents and that consequently they do not receive the hazardous-work premium implied by the theory of the perfectly functioning market. Employers, therefore, would not be motivated to provide optimal amounts of prevention.

For this argument to be valid, all workers hired must underestimate the riskiness of the job. Perhaps many do; but to generate accurate wage premiums only a portion of the work force need be fully aware of the risks. It is the marginal employee who determines the risk premium necessary to attract the equilibrium number of workers, just as in a competitive environment with no risks it is the last worker hired who determines the wage. If, in order to attract enough workers, the employer must hire some workers who have accurate perceptions, the wage for all workers will reflect this accurate perception. This is because an employer is generally unable to discriminate among workers as to their wages if the only difference is their risk perceptions.[6]

The competitive process of wage determination does not, of course, guarantee that the equilibrium wage rate will correctly reflect

---

[6] J. R. Hicks, *The Theory of Wages*, 2d ed. (New York: St. Martin's Press, 1966), pp. 110-11, describes lack of knowledge about risks as one reason market determination of the quantity of safety is not likely to be optimal. A study of natural disasters also suggests that individuals underestimate risks. Howard Kunreuther, *Recovery from Natural Disasters* (Washington, D.C.: American Enterprise Institute for Public Policy Research, 1973), p. 27. The details of the argument that it is the marginal rather than the average employee who determines the wage are explained in Milton Friedman, *Price Theory, A Provisional Text* (Chicago: Aldine, 1962), pp. 199-225.

risks unless the last person hired has the correct perception of the job's riskiness. It does demonstrate, however, that the presence of some workers who underestimate risk does not doom the market adjustment process to this inaccuracy. It must also be remembered that the wage-determination process is not limited to the initial hiring stage, and that the longer an employee is on the job, the less he is likely to underestimate the risks. Labor market institutions such as unions may also aid the information generating process.

If private markets do not achieve optimal control of accidents and disease because of inadequate information about risk, several alternatives are available. The government might require disclosure of each firm's injury record [7] or place liability for employees' accident costs on the firm. The latter system would reduce the need for information, since the difference in effective risk among firms would be eliminated. Unfortunately, even this latter alternative is not without difficulties. By eliminating the costs of accidents to employees it may reduce their incentive to avoid accidents.

The government safety rules approach also requires extensive information to operate effectively. A government agency needs information about the nature of risks and prevention at individual workplaces. This may be especially difficult since government inspectors are not party to the employer/employee relationship at the workplace.

The system of liability assignment based on court determinations of fault might also suffer from problems arising from lack of information. Uncertainty about the law or court rulings may lead both employers and employees to gamble on not being held liable. This would only be a problem, however, if it were not clear which party could most efficiently have prevented an accident or disease.

Bargaining. In an efficient situation, accidents and diseases would be prevented by the party for whom the cost of doing so was the least. The cost of bargaining among parties to achieve this efficiency is another complication. Bargaining costs include searching for the least costly preventer, trading obligations, and enforcing contracts.[8]

---

[7] Before the enactment of workmen's compensation, the employer had a common law duty to provide the employee with information about certain risks. This duty was limited to a "warning of dangers of which the employee might reasonably be expected to remain in ignorance" (W. L. Prosser, *Law of Torts*, p. 526).

[8] These negotiating costs are not limited to the employee-employer relationship. Since safe behavior by one employee has implications for other employees' safety, bargaining may occur among employees. In economic literature the costs of bargaining and information gathering are known as transactions costs. The notion is that these costs are necessary to consummate an exchange of rights and obligations among parties.

If one party is the least costly preventer of most potential accidents and diseases, assignment of liability to this party would minimize these costs. For example, if there are significant economies of scale in accident prevention, the employer is likely to be the least costly preventer of most accidents.

One problem that is especially difficult to overcome by bargaining is the occurrence of accidents through employee carelessness. In the theoretical discussion it was assumed that employee carelessness could be controlled and optimized by costless ancillary bargains and that these bargains could also be enforced at no cost. In the actual employment relationship, however, these costs are greater than zero—perhaps very high.[9] If employee carelessness is a significant factor in producing accidents, the assignment of liability to the employer is likely to generate more accidents than would other arrangements, for two reasons. First, the employer is essentially providing insurance for accident costs, thereby reducing the employees' reward for avoiding accidents. Second, the employer may be unable to induce employee care efficiently because of the associated bargaining costs.

The problem of reduced incentives for self-protective behavior induced by insurance protection is known as a moral hazard.[10] This problem may occur even under employee liability. If employees use the hazardous-work premiums to save against future losses, the equilibrium level of care would not appear to be influenced because the full cost of carelessness would be borne by the employee. However, if employees choose to use their wage premiums to buy market insurance, a potential inducement to carelessness (a moral hazard) could develop because the insured individual may not incur the full costs of careless behavior. This induced carelessness could be reduced if insurance costs can be made a function of careless behavior.

Under employer liability, the employee is essentially forced to buy insurance against accident costs, thereby creating a potential moral hazard. A firm that insures its liability in the market would also be subject to a moral hazard to the extent that its careless behavior is not taken into account in the premium. However, a self-

---

[9] The difficulty of enforcing safety rules on uncooperative employees is demonstrated in three OSHA cases in which the employers had rules but the employees refused to follow them. Industrial Steel Erectors, Inc., Occupational Safety and Health Review Commission, OSHRC Docket No. 703, August 30, 1972; Babcox and Wilcox Construction Co., OSHRC Docket No. 3208, September 20, 1973; Cam Industries, Inc., OSHRC Docket No. 258, March 4, 1974.

[10] For a discussion of insurance and moral hazards, see Isaac Ehrlich and Gary Becker, "Market Insurance, Self-Insurance, and Self-Protection," *Journal of Political Economy*, vol. 80 (1972), pp. 623-48. As used here, the word *moral* is quite without its usual connotations.

insured firm would have no related disincentive to accident and disease prevention since it fully bears the costs of its carelessness.[11]

Carelessness could best be discouraged by a system of tort liability, under which it is the basis for a finding of negligence. The costs of administering such a system might be large, if the law requires a determination of negligence in each case. However, a formal legal proceeding is not usually required for every case under a stable common law system. Whatever the legal costs, however, their amount is not an accurate measure of the efficiency of the system. It is the net value of all costs and benefits rather than one particular cost that must be considered.[12] Even when substantial expenditures are needed to determine fault, tort liability is sometimes viewed as the system likely to be most efficient. For example, in situations where the costs of making ancillary bargains with the efficient preventer are high, such as when employees are not under the direct supervision of the employer, the fault system may minimize total costs since it eliminates the need for such agreements. If the common law standards for determining fault are based on the relative efficiency of each party in the various phases of prevention, the need for ancillary bargains would be reduced. Where both parties can prevent an accident, a system of liability based on contributory negligence may be the most efficient. The causes of industrial accidents, however, are extremely difficult to determine. Published analyses have been unable to approach agreement about them, even within such broad categories as environmental and behavioral causes.[13]

If the costs of enforcing liability assignments or private agreements are very high, it may be desirable to avoid these enforcement costs by the use of government fiat. In some situations the costs of enforcing a fiat may be substantially less than the costs of determining liability. For example, consider the problem of carelessly discarded flip-top can openers. These openers may cause injuries to people who step on them with bare feet. As a social goal, it would be desirable to prevent these injuries if they can be prevented at a cost lower than the cost of the injuries. One remedy might be the assignment of injury costs to the can manufacturers or the consumer of the can's contents; however, it would be very expensive to track down the party with liability. Even if it were relatively easy to identify the

---

[11] The presence of a moral-hazard cost does not imply that insurance is undesirable any more than legal costs necessarily make the tort system undesirable. See generally, Harold Demsetz, "Information and Efficiency: Another Viewpoint," *Journal of Law and Economics*, vol. 12 (1969), p. 1.

[12] Benham, "The Effect of Advertising," pp. 337-52.

[13] See chapter 1, pp. 8-9.

can manufacturer or the consumer, it would be difficult for those parties to enforce an appropriate amount of care on the part of those who *might* be injured. In this case, such care would be wearing shoes in potentially hazardous situations. The optimal policy in this situation might be a fiat which prohibited flip-top openers. Such a policy is not without its own substantial costs, such as the forgone convenience of such openers and the loss of freedom associated with an absolute prohibition. I have no information as to the actual injury costs or consumer benefits attributable to such openers; however, if injury costs are substantial, the enforcement difficulties of liability assignments might make a mandatory rule the optimal policy.

Barriers. Legal barriers to the transfer of rights and liabilities are another cause of friction that may be detrimental to the accident optimization process. If for some reason a policy results in a non-optimal allocation of safety resources, the parties may be able to rectify this by agreement unless prohibited by the overall legal arrangement. For example, an employer under a tort system may find that his costs, which include legal fees, are much higher than they would be under a system where he guaranteed all accident costs for his employees. Accident costs themselves may be higher under a tort system because of the uncertainty of the rulings from case to case. Here his employees may be willing to exchange their right to a risky court hearing with a potentially large payoff for a guaranteed smaller amount of accident compensation. Restrictions on such trade-offs do exist, although they are clearly against the interests of both parties. For example, individuals are not allowed to exchange their workers' compensation benefits for a tort recovery or a preinjury cash payment, and exculpatory clauses are frequently not enforceable.

Bureaucratic Goals. Another difficulty with the mechanisms of accident control may come from bureaucratic goals. In describing the workings of an ideal system of control by fiat, we assumed that the goal of the bureaucracy was to require safety prevention efforts up to the point where the returns to prevention equal the costs of prevention. In practice, however, bureaucracies can only promulgate undiscriminating general regulations that cannot achieve this end. Costs and returns vary with each firm, so it is unlikely that typical bureaucratic rules will be optimal for either the firm or its employees. It is also unlikely that government inspectors enforcing the fiat mechanism will be familiar with the least-cost method of achieving a goal in a specific firm. The current OSHA system is an example of this distortion. This agency, which uses compulsory safety rules and inspectors, has virtually ignored worker actions as a factor in prevention. Its elaborate rules concentrate almost exclusively on the physical environment of the workplace.

Summary. The following table summarizes the alternatives available for regulating occupational safety and health. It should be emphasized that an optimal policy might include elements of some or all of these prototypes.

Analysis illustrates that the impact of each control mechanism depends upon its complications in everyday practice. Although we can speculate on the nature and extent of these complications, it is impossible to arrive at a purely theoretical assessment of their quantitative importance. How much information is required to generate a reasonably accurate system of wage differentials so as to impose employees' accident costs on the firm? How high can the administrative costs of a tort system be before it becomes uneconomic? How far can the bureaucracy's actions deviate from economic efficiency before they become an obstacle to safety? How important is carelessness as a factor in accidents? The answers to such questions cannot be deduced from theory. Nor are they easily found through direct empirical examination of the costs of transacting; measurement of these factors does not appear to be feasible. Even if practical complications could be measured, there is no standard available by which to judge their significance. Therefore, insight into the workings of alternative control mechanisms can apparently be gained only by determination of their influence on the allocation of resources. There is an abundance of literature on industrial safety and health regulation, yet little attention has been paid to the fact that only empirical analysis can resolve the debate over the true cost/benefit impact of alternative systems in practice. The remainder of this chapter will analyze some of these alternative systems.

Empirical Evidence on Safety Regulation

In the abstract world of perfectly functioning institutions, the manner in which accident-cost liability is assigned has little influence on prevention incentives and, therefore, little impact on the incidence of accidents and disease. However, practical complications under alternative systems of liability assignment may distort the incentives to accident prevention. Therefore empirical analysis of the actual impact of alternative systems is required to choose an appropriate public policy. There are no theoretical shortcuts.

Table 1
PUBLIC POLICY ALTERNATIVES

	Strict Liability on Employees	Strict Liability on Employers	Shared Strict Liability	Liability Based on Fault	Government Safety Rules	Income Security Financed by Payroll Taxes
Description	Employees are initially liable for all of their accident costs.	Employers are initially liable for all accident costs.	Employers are automatically liable for a portion of employee accident costs.	Whichever party is negligent is liable.	Government safety rules enforced by inspectors and fines	Those unable to work because of industrial accidents are supported by payroll tax revenues.
Achievement of Safety Objective	May not give optimal prevention incentives to employers	May not give optimal prevention incentives to employees	Uncertain	Specific incentives to all parties if legal system operates efficiently	Uncertain	Would distort both employee and employer prevention incentives
Achievement of Income Security Goal	No mandatory income security	Full income security	Substantial income security	No mandatory income security for negligent workers	No mandatory income security	Full income security
Other Considerations			Basically like the current workers' compensation system	Administrative costs may be high. This is the legal system used for most nonwork accidents.	Requires an extensive bureaucracy to enforce rules	Administrative costs would probably be relatively low.

43

Fault versus Strict Liability. One of the issues most basic to public policy is the difference, if any, in accident prevention incentives between a system based on determinations of fault and a system of automatic or strict liability like workers' compensation.[14] The fault system is currently used for assigning liability for most nonoccupational injuries, but it is extremely difficult to compare it with workers' compensation. The myriad factors underlying occupational versus nonoccupational injuries make it impossible to isolate the impact of the legal system. There is, however, a historical basis for comparing the two systems, since the fault system was used to deal with occupational injuries immediately before the adoption of workers' compensation. Evaluating the periods before and after the change to workers' compensation permits us to hold many of the accident-producing factors constant and thereby isolate the impact of regulatory policy.

Ideally, the standard for evaluating the legal systems should be the degree to which they contribute to the achievement of an optimal quantity of risk, but unfortunately, no measurement of optimal risk or even the overall level of risk is available. A workable approximation of overall occupational risk is the number of deaths due to machinery accidents (other than motor-vehicle accidents) relative to the number of employees.[15] Since the states adopted workers' compensation at different times, there must be a correction for accident-producing factors that might vary over time, such as business cycles, medical technology, and the extent of mechanization. These factors can be taken into account by measuring risk as a ratio of the experience of a particular state in a particular year relative to the average experience for the whole country. Thus, factors like medical technology, which could be expected to influence death rates but which are not likely to have a differential impact on individual states, do not need to be directly considered.

In the analysis, death rates for the five-year period before workers' compensation were compared with the five-year period after workers' compensation. Three-year averages were also analyzed. The statistical technique used was multiple regression where the dependent variable was the death rate and the key independent variable was the absence or presence of workers' compensation. As shown in table 2, the results clearly indicate that the death rate declined after workers' compensation was instituted as the remedy for accident costs. The same result was obtained when the time of observations was extended to all years for which data were available in the period 1900 to 1940.

---

[14] Even though a worker's injury must meet the standards of compensability discussed in chapter 2, the employer's liability without regard to fault makes workers' compensation a form of strict liability.

[15] Appendix B describes the data, statistical techniques, and results of this analysis.

Table 2

IMPACT OF LEGAL CHANGE ON DEATH RATES: AS
MEASURED BY THE WORKERS' COMPENSATION (*WC*)
COEFFICIENT

3 Year Pre/Post Averages	5 Year Pre/Post Averages
WC	*WC*
-0.19[a]	-0.32[a]
(-3.7)	(-4.8)
$R^2 = 0.96, F = 11.26$[a]$, n = 52$	$R^2 = 0.91, F = 4.7$[a]$, n = 42$

[a] Significant at the 1 percent level. Numbers in parentheses are *t* values. The coefficients were estimated using multiple regression with a dummy variable reflecting the presence or absence of workers' compensation. The details of the analysis are described in Appendix B.

Source: James Robert Chelius, "Liability for Industrial Accidents: A Comparison of Negligence and Strict Liability Systems," *Journal of Legal Studies*, vol. 5, no. 2 (June 1976), pp. 291–309.

Although this analysis implies that strict liability is a means of reducing the accidental death rate and presumably the overall level of risk, it does not imply that this result is optimal. It is possible that this remedy discouraged high-risk activities that had compensating benefits. By measuring only risks and not benefits, the analysis cannot guarantee that lower levels of risk associated with workers' compensation represent a more desirable situation. It does, however, provide insight into the level of risk prevailing under each system—an issue of great importance that has in the past been debated largely on the basis of anecdotes.

Even if we accept the notion that the lower level of risk makes workers' compensation superior to alternative arrangements, we still require information about the most desirable internal structure for the system. The proportion of accident costs for which the employer is to be strictly liable is obviously a crucial issue. To gain insight into this issue, the impact of benefit levels (the proportion of costs for which the employer is liable) was analyzed.

The Impact of Benefit Levels. One of the key issues of workers' compensation is the impact of benefits on incentives for safe behavior. The only way to evaluate this is to measure the relationship between benefit levels and safety. Here again it is necessary to correct for a multitude of accident-producing factors in order to isolate the impact of benefit levels. The research design chosen to measure this relationship was a cross section of manufacturing industries in various states for the year 1967.[16] This year was chosen because of the wide range of data available. In each of the eighteen states with available data, the manufacturing sector was divided into seventeen relatively homogeneous groups.[17] The injury rate and workers'-compensation benefit levels were calculated for each of the state industry groups. Other factors taken into account included demographic characteristics of the labor force and economic characteristics of the industries.

The results of the analysis clearly indicate that higher workers' compensation benefits are not associated with lower injury rates. On the contrary, higher benefit levels were associated with higher injury rates. Although the positive correlation between these variables does not demonstrate a causal relationship, such a relationship is by no means implausible. A more generous workers' compensation system reduces the worker's injury cost; it is not unreasonable to assume that he will therefore have less incentive to avoid risky activity. It is unlikely that higher benefits induce workers consciously to exercise less care in undertaking activities which directly involve the risk of serious injury. It may be that workers more readily undertake activities they perceive to have only minor risks. Unfortunately, "minor" risks sometimes lead to serious injuries. Another plausible explanation for the association of higher benefits and higher injuries, not exclusive of the first, is that more generous benefits encourage workers to report injuries that would otherwise be ignored. The system used to measure injury rates makes this rationalization unlikely but not impossible. This explanation would be consistent with experience under strict liability systems used to handle automobile accidents.[18]

Evidence on Other Systems. This section briefly summarizes the research on other issues relevant to evaluating alternative safety policies. As noted in chapter 1, the best available research indicates that employees and employers are both responsible for a substantial portion of accidents. Since the OSHA system has largely ignored the worker's role in accident and disease prevention, the effectiveness of such a regulatory effort is inherently limited.

In his study bearing on the fiat approach, Paul Sands examined the effectiveness of compulsory controls in the construction industry

---

[16] Details of the research are presented in Appendix C.

[17] The two-digit groupings of the Standard Industrial Classification system were the industry categories used. Most states did not have all industries.

[18] "Who's to Blame," *Barron's* (January 26, 1976), p. 7.

in Michigan and Ohio.[19] Sands felt that for the pre-OSHA period covered in the analysis, 1960 to 1963, these states represented "opposite extremes insofar as the amount of government influence on and control of safety activities." Sands's perception of diversity between the two states at that time is reinforced by my examination of the safety budgets and inspection staffs in each state. Ohio's safety budget amounted to $0.63 for each nonagricultural worker per year while Michigan's allocation was $0.20. The number of safety inspectors per 100,000 population of working age came to 1.3 in Ohio and 0.6 in Michigan.[20]

Rather than rely on published statistics, which he felt were unreliable, Sands personally gathered data from twenty-five construction firms in each state. His analysis of the data was limited to a simple comparison of the frequency rate of injuries in the Michigan and the Ohio firms. He found that although the injury rate was lower in Ohio, the difference was not significant. Based on this finding he concluded, "the construction safety legislation and the safety services and enforcement provided by the state government in Ohio do not result in a significantly lower rate of injuries or seem to promote increased safety precautions."

Because of the limited scope of the data, the less than complete adjustment for other factors, and the absence of statistical rigor, the results of this study cannot be taken as conclusive. However, they do cast doubt on the effectiveness of government control using mandatory safety standards.

My own work indicates that the more comprehensive, better funded state industrial safety programs in the pre-OSHA period had no more impact than the weak programs.[21] Most supporters of mandatory standards will argue that all state programs prior to OSHA were weak; even if this were true, however, one would still expect that the relatively more rigorous state programs would perform better. My research involved consideration of four dimensions of each of thirteen state laws, specifically, (1) the safety budget per nonagricultural worker, (2) the number of inspectors per nonagricultural establish-

---

[19] Paul E. Sands, "How Effective is Safety Legislation?" *The Journal of Law and Economics*, vol. 11 (April 1968), pp. 165-79.
[20] U.S. Congress, Senate, Subcommittee on Labor of the Senate Committee on Labor and Public Welfare, *Hearings on the Occupational Safety and Health Act of 1970* (testimony of Jerome Gordon), 91st Congress, 2d sess., part 1 (1970), p. 214.
[21] Chelius, "The Control of Industrial Accidents," pp. 700-29.

ment, (3) an index of the extensiveness of the safety standards, and (4) an index of the strictness of safety standards. After correcting for other relevant factors, a composite index of these attributes was found to be unrelated to the injury rates in manufacturing establishments, although there was some indication that the more rigorous standards systems may have reduced the injury rate in very large establishments. In 1967, the year for which data were collected, the sample states' expenditures for standards regulation ranged from zero to $0.84 per nonagricultural employee. In 1974, after correcting for inflation, the OSHA budget amounted to $1.15 (1967 dollars) per nonagricultural employee. Perhaps this type of regulation will become effective with higher expenditures, but one cannot be optimistic.

Direct comparisons of the level of industrial safety immediately before and after OSHA are difficult to make because the injury data system changed as the law went into effect. Robert Smith in part circumvented this problem by comparing the before and after injury records in industries that were given special attention by OSHA.[22] By this means it is possible to determine whether the special attention by OSHA improved safety. According to Smith's analysis, it did not; no positive results were indicated from the early and vigorous enforcement of OSHA standards.

Conclusions

It is difficult to be optimistic about the effects of government safety regulation. The only substantial evidence of beneficial impact is that the shared-strict-liability system of workers' compensation was associated with a higher level of safety than the system based on determination of negligence. Although workers' compensation may be a useful legal device for governing work injuries, the evidence on benefit levels demonstrates that it is important to consider the internal structure of that system. Simply lowering all benefits is not a proper means of reforming workers' compensation, since this would lower the employer's incentives for safety and compromise the income-security goal. There are, however, possible changes that could alleviate the disincentive to safety of high across-the-board benefits with minimal effect on employers' prevention incentives and the crucial aspects of income security. Unfortunately, none of the proposed reforms of the system have dealt satisfactorily with this issue. It is to a review of these proposals that we now turn.

---

[22] Robert Smith, *The Occupational Safety and Health Act* (Washington, D.C.: American Enterprise Institute, 1976), pp. 97-104.

4
PROPOSED REFORMS OF THE WORKERS' COMPENSATION SYSTEM

As part of the Occupational Safety and Health Act of 1970, Congress established a National Commission to examine the state liability systems for industrial accidents and diseases. The commission evaluated these systems and made recommendations for extensive changes.[1] Although the commission's *Report* (1972) urged the individual states to adopt its recommendations, federal action was suggested in case the states failed to comply by 1975. Since 1972, the states have substantially changed their workers' compensation laws; however, no state has adopted all of the recommendations. In response Senators Harrison Williams and Jacob Javits introduced legislation in 1975 that would establish federal minimum standards for the workers' compensation system in every state. These proposed federal standards go far beyond the standards recommended by the National Commission.

The Commission's Recommendations

The commission's *Report* contains detailed and extensive recommendations, the essence of which is to continue the shared liability system embodied in current workers' compensation laws but with expanded coverage and substantial increases in injury benefits. Specifically, the commission recommended that each state make its law compulsory for virtually all employers and employees. Traditional exemptions for such groups as farm workers, domestics, government employees, and professional athletes would be eliminated. Furthermore, the commission urged the inclusion of small firms, which are now often exempted. To expand the system further, the commission suggested that all work-related diseases be covered.

---

[1] *The Report of the National Commission on State Workmen's Compensation Laws* (Washington, D.C., 1972).

In what is probably the most significant recommendation, the commission urged a substantial increase in the benefits paid to workers. It favors a reduction of the waiting period to a maximum of three days and retroactive payment of the benefits covering that period if the worker's disability lasts fourteen or more days. The level of benefits for deaths and for temporary and permanent total disabilities is to be at least 80 percent of the worker's spendable earnings, subject to a maximum weekly benefit.[2] The maximum benefit is to be at least 100 percent of the state's average weekly wage immediately and is to increase to 200 percent by 1981. It was also recommended that there be no limit on total benefits except as the result of a change in a dependent's status through remarriage or upon reaching majority.[3]

The basic thrust of the commission's recommendations is to create a workers' compensation system more congruent with maintaining the income of injured workers. Unfortunately, as we have seen in both theory and practice, there is a conflict between the accomplishment of the income-maintenance goal and the encouragement of safety. The commission's *Report* acknowledges the encouragement of safety as one of the objectives of workers' compensation but offers litte more than a generalized hope that higher benefits will somehow encourage employers to prevent more accidents. How workers might be encouraged to prevent accidents is not discussed at all.

As examples of the commission's minimal attention to safety encouragement, consider its specific recommendations in the area of accident and disease prevention.[4] For one, it recommends "that insurance carriers be required to provide loss prevention services and that the workmens' compensation agency carefully audit the services."[5] This recommendation is made because some insurance companies do not offer prevention services as part of their insurance service. "In some states there are more than 100 carriers writing workmen's compensation insurance. It is unlikely that they are all able to provide effective and comprehensive safety programs."[6] It is neither appro-

---

[2] Spendable earnings are gross wages adjusted for federal income and social security taxes. They do not include an adjustment for fringe benefits.

[3] Appendix D contains a complete statement of the commission's eighty-four recommendations.

[4] These recommendations are from The Report of the National Commission, chapter 5, "The Safety Objective," pp. 87-98.

[5] The Report of the National Commission, p. 93.

[6] The Report of the National Commission, p. 93. As noted in Nicholas Ashford, Crisis in the Workplace: Occupational Disease and Injury (Cambridge: MIT Press, 1976), p. 490, the largest writer of workers' compensation insurance (Liberty Mutual) in 1971 ". . . had more technical personnel than OSHA had compliance officers. Furthermore, in 1970, Liberty Mutual Loss Prevention made 132,829 visits to policy holders, versus only 14,800 inspections by OSHA in its first two years."

priate nor desirable for all insurance companies to offer comprehensive prevention services. An employer desiring them can simply contract with a firm that does offer the service. Other employers will not want prevention services from an insurance company if they and their employees are satisfied with the safety efforts already being made. Employers may also hire one of the many safety consulting firms that offers prevention services without insurance. The important objective is to give employers and employees the incentive to be safe. Requiring all insurance carriers to provide safety services is presumptuous and wasteful. Employers and insurance companies will not obey such a rule unless they are coerced. An additional layer of bureaucracy would therefore be needed to enforce this economically inefficient arrangement.

The same lack of substance is embodied in the recommendation that "subject to sound actuarial standards, the experience rating principle be extended to as many employers as practicable."[7] Although it is beneficial to price insurance policies on the individual characteristics of each firm, the administrative costs of doing so may be prohibitive. Small firms have so few employees and so few accidents that an insurer cannot reliably estimate his future liabilities. Many small employers currently pay workers' compensation insurance premiums that reflect the risks of their industry group, with no adjustment for their own experience. For larger employers, the benefits of individual pricing may be worth the extra administrative costs. Surely the decision process is governed by the simple economics of costs and benefits. Since the costs of such an extension outweigh the benefits, there is nothing socially undesirable in allowing insurance companies to price some policies on industry rather than firm characteristics. The commission has proclaimed the benefits of experience rating while ignoring the costs.

Two other "safety" recommendations were made by the commission. A useful one was to merge the workers' compensation and Occupational Safety and Health Administration injury-data bases. The other was merely a variation of the recommendation to extend the use of experience ratings.

The recommendations of the commission are easily summarized: maintaining the current system of shared strict liability, extending its use to more employers and employees, and increasing the employer's share of liability via higher benefits. As noted, however, scant attention is paid to substantive policies affecting safety incentives. If workers' compensation does not contribute to the goal of optimal

---

[7] *The Report of the National Commission*, p. 98.

safety, what reason can there be for having a system that separates occupational injuries from the multitude of other reasons for inadequate income?

The Congressional Proposals for Reform

In June 1975, Senators Javits and Williams introduced the National Workers' Compensation Act.[8] The purpose of the bill is to establish federal minimum standards for all state workers' compensation laws. While the act was inspired by *The Report of the National Commission,* many of its provisions differ substantially from the commission's recommendations. None of the differences bears directly on the conflict between income maintenance and efficient accident and disease prevention that dominated our discussion of the commission's recommendations, but they strongly influence the stability and generosity of the system. This, in turn, could seriously hamper the usefulness of the workers' compensation system.

Since this bill or one of its descendants is likely to be the mechanism for putting federal power behind the commission's recommendations, it is important to examine its provisions. Some aspects of the bill are objectionable even to those who strongly support the workers' compensation system and federal efforts to implement the commission's proposed changes.[9] The act proposes standards that are potentially counterproductive to its objectives. Under the current system, covered injuries are those which have arisen out of and in the course of employment. Within each state, case law has yielded standards that define the boundaries of this condition. Concepts such as "positional risk" and "street risk" are among the criteria used to provide guidance.[10] Each party's or his attorney's knowledge of these definitions

---

[8] S.2018, 94th Congress, 1st session (1975). Senators Javits and Williams introduced the bill on behalf of themselves and Senators Pell, Kennedy, Humphrey, Mondale, Hathaway, and Cranston. The companion House bill was H.R. 9431. A later proposal, H.R. 2058, the "National Workers' Compensation Standards Act of 1977," was introduced by Congressman Joseph M. Gaydos (D-Pa.).

[9] The following discussion is based in part on a speech by Arthur Larson, the author of the leading legal treatise on workers' compensation, before the National Council of Self-Insurers held at Salt Lake City on September 7, 1975. The speech was entitled, "S.2018 as a Vehicle for Workmen's Compensation Reform." Further material was obtained from the testimony of John F. Burton, Jr. before the Subcommittee on Labor of the Senate Committee on Labor and Public Welfare, March 3, 1976. Burton was the chairman of the National Commission on State Workmen's Compensation Laws.

[10] Web Malone, Marcus Plant, and Joseph Little, *The Employment Relation* (St. Paul: West Publishing, 1974), pp. 1-514, has an extensive description of these and other doctrines that have become established by the case law of workers' compensation.

greatly helps to achieve a low cost of administration, one of the advantages of workers' compensation. Since each party is aware of the criteria, there is a minimal need for court proceedings to determine whether an injury falls within the standard. The National Commission recommended that an injury's "arising out of and in the course of employment" continue to be a test for coverage. The Williams-Javits bill states that "[an] 'injury' shall be deemed to have arisen out of and in the course of employement *if work-related factors were a significant cause of the injury.*" [11] The addition of "significant cause" as a qualifying condition would mean a complete relitigation of the body of case law on this issue. There is no legal or common use of the word *significant* that makes its meaning obvious in this context. The dictionary states that something significant is important or momentous. One interpretation is that the new test is intended to extend coverage to a greater number of injuries, but it is not clear that the inevitable litigation on this issue would yield such a result.

As an example of the potential restrictions on coverage made possible by the enactment of such a phrase, consider the doctrine of "positional risk." Some states currently use this test to determine compensation where an injury is the result of a hazard that also affects the general public. For instance, if the worker's job required him to be at a particular place at a particular time, then the injury is found to have arisen out of and in the course of employment. Arthur Larson offers the case of a man "standing in a factory when a beetle flies into his eye. [N]o one in his right mind would say that the employment was an 'important' cause of that injury." [12] Such an injury would now be compensated under the positional risk test, but the language of the proposed statute with its emphasis on "cause" would probably deny compensation. This may not be the intended result of the statute, but the use of legally ambiguous terms such as "significant cause" makes it difficult to determine what the intent is. It is hard to imagine why the proposed coverage test is deemed an improvement, why it is necessary as a federal standard, or even whether it will result in broader or narrower coverage.

A similar change is proposed for the definition of disability. Case law has established reasonably stable concepts of disability in each state. The proposed legislation would throw the established concepts of disability into confusion by including any one of the following:

---

[11] Emphasis added. Section 3(7) of the bill. S.2008 introduced in 1974 by Senators Williams and Javits provided that the test be whether work-related factors were a "contributing cause" of the injury.

[12] Larson, "S.2018," p. 13.

(1) incapacity to perform or obtain work suitable to the employee's qualifications and training;

(2) incapacity to earn the wages which the employee was receiving at the time of a work-related injury; *or* [emphasis added],

(3) incapacity for future work and wages.[13]

It is not clear what is intended by such a definition, but it must be something other than the current concepts since it does not use the standard language. Again the new definition will lead to extensive litigation concerning its meaning if the bill is enacted, introducing further uncertainty into the system. One of the prime virtues of workers' compensation is supposed to be its certainty. Arthur Larson has criticized this definition, pointing out that the use of "or" before the phrase "incapacity for future work and wages" means that this part of the definition is intended as a separate concept of disability. But what does it mean?

> What is "incapacity"? Is it incapacity to perform work, or to obtain it? What kind of work? Must it, as in the first part of the definition, be suitable to the employee's qualifications and training? If so, why was this not put in part three as well as in part one? And what does "future" mean? How far in the future and for how long? And what in the world is "incapacity for wages"? What kind of wages, and with what relation to previous wages or earning capacity? I can readily imagine a number of claimants, unable to meet normal standards of disability proof, nevertheless going into court and relying on "incapacity for future work and wages," on the theory that this must mean something different from the kind of incapacity described earlier in the definition.[14]

The Senators, having proposed a new litigation-prone version of workers' compensation, then propose that their system be mandatory for all employees except those covered by other federal legislation.[15] Household and casual workers would be covered. This means that a prudent "employer" who did nothing more than hire a babysitter once a month would have to purchase workers' compensation insurance. The National Commission recognized the administrative problems that would be posed by extensive coverage. Its recommendation was to

---

[13] Emphasis added. S.2018, p. 7.

[14] Larson, "S.2018," pp. 13-14.

[15] Railroad employees, federal government employees, and seamen have separate legislation. See chapter 2, pp. 19-22 for a discussion.

cover workers only to the extent that they were covered by social security.[16]

Beyond any qualms one might have about the recommendations of the National Commission, passage of the National Workers' Compensation Act or similar legislation would create many problems that would counteract some of the advantages of the workers' compensation approach to industrial-accident-liability law. Workers' compensation may not assign the liability in an optimal manner but it has the virtue of stability and relative ease of administration—one of the important goals of any liability system. Stability allows employers and employees to work out arrangements that at least in part offset any inefficiencies introduced by legislation. The new and arbitrary definitions, such as proposed by the act can only detract from the present stability and give rise to extensive litigation in an effort to define terms such as *disability* and *significant cause*.[17] The added costs of such extensive coverage would also run counter to the goal of a reasonably efficient administrative system.

The act also goes beyond the recommendations of the National Commission in the generosity of its mandatory benefits. Minimum weekly benefits for those with total disabilities would be established. The proposed minimum is 50 percent of the statewide average weekly wage or 100 percent of the injured worker's weekly wage, whichever is less. Although the commission did recommend that benefits be at least 80 percent of spendable earnings and that the legal maximum on benefits not be too low, it made no mention of a minimum benefit.[18] The reason for avoiding a minimum benefit is that the requirement may force the employer to pay more in compensation and medical benefits than the financial losses suffered by the below-average-wage employee. It is not at all clear why the employer should be the one responsible for the extra financial support. The extra burden would only serve to discourage employers from hiring such workers. Furthermore, it is clear that a worker receiving benefits equal to 100 percent of his wages or more would not have as much incentive to rehabilitate himself as would be desirable.

Although not a key aspect of the bill, a clause on refusal to accept medical care illustrates the extremes embodied in the proposed

---

[16] The minimum requirement for social security coverage is that a worker earns $50 or more in wages during a three-month period.

[17] In perhaps the epitome of definitional circularity, the act defines an employee as "any individual employed by an employer." An employer is defined as "any person who employs any individual."

[18] The recommendation is that by 1981, the maximum be at least 200 percent of the state's average weekly wage. See Appendix D for the full recommendations on benefit levels.

legislation. The provision would require employers to pay benefits to workers who remain disabled solely because their religious beliefs require them to refuse medical or rehabilitative services. No one would dispute the right of an injured worker to refuse treatment, but it appears unreasonable to force the employer to finance the worker's indulgence in that belief. The limited case law on this issue under existing workers' compensation statutes implies that the employer currently would be liable for only the portion of a disability that would have existed had the worker taken the recommended medical care. Is this really such a critical aspect of industrial-accident-liability law that it must be imposed as a federal minimum standard on all states? Surely the states could be allowed to deal severally with this issue without offense to the objectives of workers' compensation or to freedom of religion. Arthur Larson has described this provision as the "most spectacularly irrelevant standard" in the Williams-Javits bill.[19]

Conclusions

The recommendations of the National Commission preserve much of what has been found workable in the current system. They rely on existing administrative procedures that are reasonably efficient. They have not changed legal definitions without apparent reason. The weaknesses of the commission's proposals lie in their near-total emphasis on income security for injured workers, a policy that can create disincentives to safety. Surely preventing accidents is as important as alleviating their financial burden when they do occur. The potentially harmful bias of the National Commission's recommendations is now being carried further by the proposed federal legislation. Income security is certainly a more politically appealing issue than efficient accident and disease prevention, and it is easy to understand its emphasis in proposals that are meant to be politically acceptable. But for appropriate policy we must also recognize the importance of creating appropriate incentives to behave in a manner which will lead to efficient accident prevention.

As we have seen throughout this analysis, a substantial liability burden on employers is not necessarily undesirable. Even if the liability includes accidents that were someone else's fault or when most might agree that the burden is in some way inequitable, strict liability to the employer may not have undesirable consequences. The key factor is not how much liability lies with a particular party but whether the structure of liability provides each party with an appropriate incentive to avoid accidents.

---

[19] Larson, "S.2018," p. 8.

The initial liability assignment will result in a direct incentive if the party who can most easily prevent accidents and diseases bears the liability. If liability is not assigned to the efficient preventer but the party with liability induces the efficient preventer to optimize safety, the incentive will be indirect but still effective. A liability assignment will not yield optimal accident and disease prevention only if the most efficient preventer is not initially liable and the party with liability cannot easily induce him to engage in the desired safe behavior. This difficulty in inducing another party to behave in a certain manner arises frequently. It occurs because employees are the efficient preventers of many accidents, especially minor accidents where the prospect of pain and suffering is not a large factor in inducing careful behavior. Unfortunately, employee behavior like horseplay, which can lead to accidents, is very difficult for employers to stop. Perhaps it could be deterred by elaborate work rules and vigilant surveillance of employees, but the cost of such a prevention effort would be much greater than the cost of a system in which each employee had an individualized incentive to behave safely. For purposes of efficient prevention it would be desirable to assign liability for such accidents to the employees. However, in pursuit of the income security goal, current systems assign employees liability for little of the loss that results from the minor injuries, most difficult for employers to prevent.

A fundamental weakness of the proposed reforms of workers' compensation is that they make the employee even less responsible for minor accident costs than the current system. A short waiting period and relatively high benefits for minor injuries create a disincentive to safe practices. Only when the burden of such minor injuries is placed more on the employee can optimal safety levels be achieved. Of course, efficient prevention is not the only policy goal; its pursuit must be constrained by concern for income security. It is to the consideration of such a reform that we now turn.

5
A PROPOSED NEW POLICY

It is clear that, in the abstract frictionless world described in chapter 3, the choice of a public policy toward industrial injuries has little effect on the encouragement of safety and health. Any of several arrangements yields essentially the same desirable results. Deficiencies in government policy will be ameliorated by private interactions in the market. We know, however, that the real world is not frictionless, and our analysis demonstrated that the choice of an optimal policy mix must be based on a consideration of the often subtle strengths and weaknesses of each alternative.

Our review of suggested reforms indicates that these proposals have not taken full account of the relative advantages and disadvantages of each system. In this final chapter we will briefly review the policy alternatives and then consider a new policy—one which could better balance the dual goals of efficient accident and disease prevention and income security. In other words, a policy will be proposed that both contributes to the prevention of accidents and diseases and compensates victims for the injuries that do occur.

A Review of the Alternatives

Although unfettered private markets are generally considered to be the most efficient method of operation within a given set of incentives, there is substantial doubt whether the correct incentives face the potential preventers of industrial injuries. Factors such as the lack of information about job risks as well as the difficulty of making and enforcing agreements about prevention responsibilities may keep the full benefits of prevention from accruing to the preventer. The denial of complete benefits to the preventer discourages him from incurring the full costs of an efficient amount of prevention. The result, then, is less than a socially desirable quantity of prevention and, hence, an undesirable quantity of accidents and diseases.

The market mechanism does not automatically guarantee income maintenance—a feature that many deem desirable. If we relied strictly on private markets, this lack of income security would also distort the allocation of prevention resources since the value judgment favoring income security will be funded by some public revenue source. Given our social values, a disabled worker will be cared for to some degree no matter how unresourceful he might have been in planning his future security and no matter how negligent he might have been in bringing about the disability. Since some income security will be provided, it ought to be a goal of public policy toward industrial accidents and disease to achieve this security in the manner that is most compatible with the goal of efficient accident and disease prevention. If an injured worker has no support during his disability, he will be eligible for support from welfare funds financed from general tax revenues. In this case a substantial portion of the injury costs would not be directly assigned to either the employee or the employer. Since accident preventers do not have these costs to be saved, there is a further incentive to engage in less prevention than is appropriate. This distortion becomes self-fulfilling since the presence of potential support from general revenues will encourage people not to provide for their own welfare in case of a disability. Thus, some degree of guaranteed income security is a necessary part of public policy toward industrial accidents and disease.

The fiat system embodied in OSHA suffers substantial weaknesses in that it requires an additional layer of bureaucracy, it is too inflexible to allow for the lowest-cost prevention in each situation, and it concentrates strictly on the employer's role in prevention. The enforcement mechanism, as in other areas of government regulation, deals with the most visible and "enforceable" aspects of the problem, which often are the most superficial and least important aspects of prevention.[1] The chief advantage of the fiat system is that it is visible

---

[1] Two regulations point out the irrelevance of many OSHA efforts toward accident and disease prevention. Murray Weidenbaum, in his *Government-Mandated Price Increases* (Washington, D.C.: American Enterprise Institute, 1975), pp. 45-47, describes his examination of the OSHA definition of an "exit": " 'Exit is that portion of a means of egress which is separated from all other spaces of the building or structure by construction or equipment as required in this subpart to provide a protected way of travel to the exit discharge.' Our typical businessman, being a persevering fellow, realizes that this subject, too, is more complicated than he had thought. Clearly, he must learn about 'means of egress' and 'exit discharge.' OSHA does not disappoint him: 'A means of egress is a continuous and unobstructed way of exit travel from any point in a building or structure to a public way and consists of three separate and distinct parts: the way of exit

politically; it satisfies the politicians' need to be able to say that "something is being done." Unfortunately, there is no evidence that any of this politically visible activity has contributed to increased overall safety, whether or not increased safety is consistent with optimal safety. The fiat system may be the only means of controlling the effects of the exotic chemical compounds used in many industries. In this case, the information and enforcement costs of a liability system may be too great to induce the proper safety incentives for employers and workers.

The tort system, in which accident costs are assigned to the party who acted negligently, also suffers from several weaknesses. The costs of obtaining a remedy through the system can be substantial, with the result that an insufficient number of cases will be adjudicated. The parties may not have the proper incentive to act carefully since they are not likely to bear the full consequences of their actions. Although every injury case need not go through a court proceeding in order to give each party the correct incentives, the costs of administering a system where this is the exclusive remedy are generally substantial. The slowness of payment inherent in a tort system also gives a bargaining advantage to the employer, since short-run cash flow problems are often far more crucial to the injured employee than to the employer. This may cause the employee to settle quickly for less than the full costs of his injury. As with other systems lacking an income guarantee, the tort system will distort the allocation of prevention resources if negligent employees are not made to suffer the effects of their carelessness.

The primary advantage of a negligence system is that, if a case is adjudicated, or if the parties agree to a settlement because they realize what the outcome of a court proceeding would be, then each party will have the proper incentives to prevent accidents and diseases. Since the goal of a fault system is to restore a victim to his condition prior to the injury and to provide a safety incentive based on the full costs of accidents, settlements have to include payments for all losses, including pain and suffering. Other than a perfectly functioning market system, a fault system, with its extensive analysis of actual

---

access; the exit; and the way of exit discharge. A means of egress comprises the vertical and horizontal ways of travel and shall include intervening room spaces, doorways, hallways, corridors, passageways, balconies, ramps, stairs, enclosures, lobbies, escalators, horizontal exits, courts, and yards.' 'Exit discharge is that portion of a means of egress between the termination of an exit and a public way.' " OSHA also recently promulgated a standard that there must be toilet and washing facilities within five minutes' walking distance of all farmworkers.

damages, offers the only hope of having the true cost of accidents including pain and suffering borne by the potential preventer.

The pain and suffering of a serious disability represent a substantial portion of the costs of an injury. It would be desirable for the legal system to assign liability for such losses so that the full cost of injuries is borne by the party in the best position to prevent the accident. The dilemma, however, is that if the awards routinely made in a workers' compensation system were to be so generous as to include pain and suffering there would be a strong incentive for employees to act with less than an optimal amount of care. As shown in chapter 3, there is some evidence that even the more generous states within the current system may fail to encourage an appropriate amount of careful employee behavior. Only a system that provides the opportunity for detailed examination of the circumstances and consequences of the injury could avoid such a distortion of incentives; but again, this would be very costly.

As shown by the evidence on death risks before and after enactment of workers' compensation laws, the cost to the employer of guaranteed benefits does appear to generate a higher level of safety than the negligence system. However, the strict liability system currently used also distorts prevention efforts, since an employer pays the same costs whether the accident results from the carelessness of the employee or his own negligence. In a situation where the employee was at fault, the employer is paying too much. In a situation where the employer was grossly negligent, his costs are too little. The compromise embodied in workers' compensation, which ignores fault, can make no distinction between these situations.

A final feature of workers' compensation worth recalling is the income security inherent in strict partial employer liability. This is certainly an advantage in achieving society's income-maintenance goal, but it can conflict with the goal of optimal prevention.

Thus we have a public policy problem in which there are several choices, each with its associated strengths and weaknesses. In response to the weaknesses of each approach, the existing policy—consisting of several programs operating simultaneously—has arisen. We have the compulsory safety rules of OSHA, the strict partial liability of workers' compensation, and the income-security supplements of social security and welfare. The haphazard development of these programs has led to a situation where the weaknesses of each approach are operating unconstrained, and the advantages of each are not fully exploited. The recommendations of the National Commission and the proposed National Workers' Compensation Act (the Williams-Javits bill) simply reinforce the weaknesses of the current system.

It is both possible and desirable to construct a policy mix which: (1) combines features of the traditional systems in an integrated rather than an ad hoc manner, and (2) deemphasizes their weaknesses and takes advantage of their strengths. It is to such an alternative that the remainder of this volume is devoted.

A Recommended Policy Mix

A policy mix based on constrained income maintenance and recognition of the workers' role in prevention can be better than the present system. The fundamental purpose of income security is to alleviate severe problems due to lack of money, not to compensate all injury costs or even to replace all lost income. It is not necessary to compensate all employee losses for all injuries to satisfy this goal. Current workers' compensation laws recognize this by replacing less than all lost income in exchange for the certainty of payment. However, the proportion of lost income replaced is typically the same for all disabilities; no distinction is made between the income-maintenance needs of a temporarily disabled worker and those of a permanently disabled worker. Surely, it is reasonable to distinguish between a sprained ankle that will heal in a few weeks and a severed hand that creates a permanent disability. Yet neither the current workers' compensation system nor the suggested reforms of the National Commission or of the Congress recognize this distinction. The National Commission recommended that all benefits be at least 80 percent of spendable earnings. The National Workers' Compensation Act (the Williams-Javits bill) would require that benefits for all injuries be 66⅔ percent of average weekly wages.

A restructuring of benefits to concentrate on serious disabilities and a corresponding deemphasis of minor injuries would achieve the fundamental purpose of income security. Such a restructuring has the advantage of reducing incentives to careless behavior and malingering, while preserving the crucial aspects of the income-security goal. This arrangement could be partially implemented by extending the waiting period for wage-loss benefits to at least two weeks. The National Commission recommended a maximum waiting period of three days. This proposed change would be analogous to increasing the deductible sum in a standard insurance policy. Wage-loss benefits for temporary disabilities could be set at minimal levels for the first few months.

63

Further restructuring could be achieved by offering substantial benefits for death and permanent total disabilities while reducing benefits for permanent partial injuries which involve no long-term wage loss.[2]

To summarize, the foundation of the first aspect of this policy is the use of a strict partial liability system. Employers would be automatically responsible for a substantial portion of wage losses resulting from serious disabilities while employees would be largely responsible for wage losses from short-term disabilities. This would provide income security for workers except in those cases where the wage loss is small. It would also provide injury-prevention incentives for both employers and employees. Because workers are faced with the prospect of a loss of wages from minor disabilities, they will be inclined to exercise care in their work. Similarly, since employers are faced with the costs of serious injuries, they also will have a substantial incentive to prevent injuries.

If employers and employees did not work out voluntary arrangements to make up for the lack of payments for pain, suffering, and partial employee responsibility for short-term income losses, employers would not pay the full cost of negligent behavior under this proposal. To counter this weakness, a modified fault system could be introduced to supplement workers' compensation.

The fault component of this system would enable workers to sue employers if they felt that their injuries were caused by serious employer negligence. In order to avoid the high cost of frequent actions under this provision, and as a quid pro quo for the employer's strict liability for serious disabilities that are not his fault, the standard for finding liability could be set higher than that of ordinary negligence. For example, a minimum standard of gross negligence could be used to establish fault. Gross negligence is usually considered to be behavior more imprudent than the simple disregard of ordinary careful-

---

[2] It is estimated that in 1973, a worker making the average wage and having the average length of disability (three weeks) would receive slightly over 50 percent of his gross wages, which probably corresponds to about 60 percent of take-home pay. Not counting the waiting period, the average benefit replaced about 70 percent of take-home pay. Since that time, several states have reduced waiting and retroactive periods and increased benefits, thus increasing the percentage of the wage replaced. The recommendation of the National Commission would yield a benefit that replaces at least 80 percent of take-home pay. Surely a 20 percent financial penalty is not a great incentive to work. This financial penalty is even less when one considers explicit costs of working such as commuting, clothing, and away-from-home meals. The source of data for 1974 was Alfred Skolnik and Daniel Price, "Workmen's Compensation Under Scrutiny," *The Social Security Bulletin* (October 1974), pp. 10-14.

ness, and may also include recklessness and intentional wrong.[3] The possibility of such a suit would serve as an incentive to the employer to avoid unsafe conduct of the sort that might be induced by the absence of strict liability for pain, suffering, and full wage losses. The restricted nature of the liability, however, would keep the number of cases to a manageable level. Since the employee would already have his workers' compensation benefits, the employer would have no special bargaining power attributable to the employee's cash flow problems.

Under this system, an employee gives up benefits during the waiting period and accepts less than full wage-loss compensation for minor disabilities in exchange for a guarantee of income regardless of who was at fault. The employer provides benefits for some injuries that are not his fault, but in the context of a system that encourages employees to act carefully and to return to work as quickly as possible. Because almost all injuries would be handled by the strict liability principle, administrative costs would be low. The small number of cases settled under the gross-negligence principle would be costly in adjudication expense but would be worth that expense because of the incentives given employers to avoid negligence. The essential element of the income-maintenance objective is achieved while each party has a substantial incentive to prevent injuries. The employee responsibility for short-term income losses virtually eliminates any disincentive to safe behavior. The possibility of a suit for full damages including pain and suffering virtually eliminates any disincentive to safe behavior by employers.

A recent situation illustrates the kind of problem with which the gross-negligence provision is designed to deal. The allegations made in this situation, whether true or false, provide an interesting case study.[4]

---

[3] Gross negligence is defined as the "intentional failure to perform a manifest duty in reckless disregard of the consequences as affecting the life or property of another; such a gross want of care and regard for the rights of others as to justify the presumption of willfulness and wantonness; . . . a manifestly smaller amount of watchfulness and circumspection than the circumstances require of a person of ordinary prudence; [or actions which are] . . . substantially higher in magnitude than simple inadvertence, but . . . short of intentional wrong." Henry Black, *Black's Law Dictionary*, 4th ed. (St. Paul: West Publishing Co., 1968), p. 1185.

[4] I have not attempted to document the allegations nor even to confirm whether news reports accurately represented the allegations. In this situation, however, the important point is not the factual accuracy of the case but the illustration it provides of reasonable possibility. Even if the news reports of the situation are incorrect, the situation is useful as a hypothetical case study. Typical news accounts are to be found in the *New York Times*, January 28, 1976, p. 14 and in the *Wall Street Journal*, August 11, 1976, p. 6.

The industrial setting was a small chemical firm which was processing Kepone for a major chemical firm. It was alleged that inadequate precautions were taken by the plant managers with the result that many of the workers and even their families became seriously ill. Thirty workers were hospitalized with tremors, blurred vision, memory loss, and possible sterility and liver cancer. A key issue in the legal proceedings has been the nature of the relationship between the major chemical company and the operation that processed the hazardous product. If the major chemical company was essentially the employer of the workers in the hazardous operation, the extent of its liability to the workers would be limited to workers' compensation benefits. If the major chemical company was not in the position of an employer but that of an independent organization hiring a contractor, the extent of its liability is determined by a court's award of actual damages. Of course, if independence characterizes their relationship, the major company would be liable only if it were found negligent—if, for example, it was aware of the hazards of processing Kepone and failed to notify the contractor. Given the large number of workers reporting substantial pain and suffering, the damages awarded in a negligence suit would probably be much greater than workers' compensation benefits.

This situation provides an insight into the potentially perverse incentives of workers' compensation. A news service alleges that while the major chemical company was publicly denying anything other than a buyer/seller relationship with the small processor, in court it was attempting to prove that it was in essence the employer of the disabled workers.[5] The advantage in demonstrating the latter relationship was a restriction on the extent of its potential liability. Thus, in a situation like this, it is clear that the strict but limited employer's liability of workers' compensation is not as strong an incentive to prevention as the threat of full damages. Yet the administrative costs and uncertainty of a system where awards in a negligence suit are the only remedy appear to make such a system undesirable. If a combined workers' compensation/gross negligence system covered the above situation, the incentive of avoiding the great cost of full damages would have operated independently of whether the major chemical company was an employer or merely a purchaser of the product. Moreover, the incentive would have existed without forgoing the advantages or workers' compensation in situations where negligence was not involved.

---

[5] CBS Television News.

Some may fear that litigation arising out of this proposal would be theoretically useful but practically troublesome. Their fears are, no doubt, influenced by the recent tremendous increases in the number and size of awards under product and professional malpractice liability. It needs to be reemphasized that the litigation made possible by this proposal is intended to be a remedy supplemental to workers' compensation and is limited to exceptional situations where the employer has grossly failed to fulfill his injury-prevention responsibilities. If such a procedure were to be used as a general supplement to workers' compensation for most disabilities, the system would degenerate into an administratively unmanageable and inefficient one.

If injury cost (whether from a product, a job, or a medical procedure) does not vary with the amount of prevention, the cost is likely to be borne by the same party no matter who has the initial liability. For example, if manufacturers are liable for the costs of injuries arising from the use of their products, the users will bear the costs in the form of an increased product price. If the user of the product is liable for such injuries, the user will not pay for the injuries in the price of the product but more directly in the cost of any injuries which he may suffer. Under such circumstances, the assignment of liability is unimportant. If we drop the assumption that costs are fixed and instead assume that they vary with the amount of prevention effort, we can reach a different conclusion—the initial liability can make a difference in the amount of prevention.

Even with variable injury costs it is possible that the assignment of liability makes no difference. However, it is necessary for the party with the initial liability to enforce safe behavior practices on the other party to the relationship. For example, consider the situation where injuries from products were largely the result of careless use of these products. If the manufacturer is liable, he must enforce safety rules by all users if he is to control the quantity of injury costs which arise from the use of his products. Since it is difficult if not impossible to enforce such rules in most situations, the quantity of injury costs will surely rise if the manufacturer has liability for all injury costs arising from the use of his product. The lesson from this example is that liability will not make any difference in prevention efforts as long as each party can bargain over the other party's safety behavior either explicitly or implicitly through refusals to work or purchase. But when such enforcement is difficult, it is necessary to have a system which directly places liability on the party who, in the absence of such liability, might not be as careful as is desirable. This is the reason for the structure of the system proposed here.

For most serious injury costs, the employer is strictly liable, thus giving the employer added incentive to avoid injuries to his employees. These guaranteed benefits will not create a disincentive for safe behavior by employees since the pain and suffering associated with most serious injuries will serve as a deterrent. Even if some careless behavior is induced by such strict liability, it is worth the price since the system offers the desirable feature of guaranteed income maintenance. Liability for short-term wage losses from minor injuries gives the employee a direct incentive to careful behavior. This eliminates the need for an enforcement mechanism by employers for the difficult-to-enforce situations. The possibility of a suit for full damages in the case of gross employer negligence eliminates the need for employees to enforce careful behavior "rules" on employers—also rules that would be extremely difficult to enforce. The proposed system, therefore, gives both employees and employers incentives to engage in the correct amount of injury prevention while providing substantial income maintenance for injured workers.

Conclusion

The combined workers' compensation/negligence policy suggested here offers reasonably accurate and clear safety incentives both to employers and to employees. Each party will suffer costs if appropriate prevention measures are not taken. The presence of these incentives would allow private parties to choose their own prevention techniques without the use of mandatory governmental rules and enforcers. Thus, the proposal takes advantage of the strengths of each system. The crucial aspect of income maintenance provided by the strict liability of workers' compensation would be preserved; the safety incentives inherent in a well-functioning fault system would be established; and the operational efficiency of the private market, once it is constrained by the proper incentives, would be achieved. All of these features are accomplished in a system which has low administrative costs because of the dominant use of strict liability.

Furthermore, several disadvantages of the traditional systems are minimized: the disincentives to safe behavior created by the overgenerosity of short-term-injury benefits would be substantially reduced; the administrative costs of the negligence system would be reduced because its use is limited to cases of gross negligence; and the income-maintenance deficiencies of the unrestrained private market and standard fault systems would be alleviated.

The major weakness of this proposal is its lack of political appeal. By eliminating the use of most mandatory governmental safety rules and a bureaucracy to enforce those rules, the system loses its visibility. Just as wage and price controls periodically emerge as a device to signal that "something is being done" about inflation, so perhaps must extensive standards remain a politically necessary aspect of government safety policy. However, what is claimed to be political reality should not deter us from recognizing the workplace realities of occupational safety and health. Income security and optimal prevention through economic encouragement of safe practices and behavior are both important objectives, the achievement of which deserves our concern and effort.

APPENDIX A

Statistical Evidence on Changes
in Injury Rates over Time

Industrial injury rates have generally been declining since the 1920s. During the 1960s, however, injury rates tended to increase. This increase was one of the principal reasons given for the passage of the Occupational Safety and Health Act of 1970. The act created federal mandatory safety rules and led to the proposals for workers' compensation reform.

It is important to know whether this increase in the 1960s represented a new problem or whether it was simply the result of forces which had existed all along. By creating OSHA, Congress demonstrated its belief that the increasing injury rate in the 1960s represented a new situation—one that supposedly required new solutions in the form of increased federal involvement. According to the following analysis, however, virtually all of the increase can be explained by changes in the level of business activity and in the age composition of the labor force. In other words, there was no evidence of a new problem in the 1960s. This appendix details the statistical analysis that led to this conclusion.

The analysis used the work of Professor Robert Smith as a starting point.[1] The first step was to estimate the relationship between work-injury rates and the business cycle as suggested by Smith. This equation was estimated using linear regression analysis. It appears in table A-1 as equation (1). As evidenced by the R^2 adjusted for the degrees of freedom, the model of economic factors explained 41 percent of the year-to-year variations in injury rates.

The second step was to augment this model of economic factors by introducing a variable for the change in the percentage of workers aged eighteen to thirty-five. The equation estimating this relationship appears as

---

This appendix is summarized from a revised version of James Robert Chelius, "The Occupational Safety and Health Problem: An Economic and Demographic Analysis," presented at the Annual Meeting of the American Public Health Association, Miami Beach, Florida, October 1976. Robert St. Onge, Jr., provided very helpful assistance in the development of this analysis.

[1] Robert S. Smith, "Intertemporal Changes in Work Injury Rates," *Proceedings of the Industrial Relations Research Association* (1973), pp. 167-74.

equation (2) in table A-1. The addition of the age variable raised the adjusted R^2 to 53 percent.

In order to determine whether the factors associated with increased injury rates in the period 1964 through 1970 were the same as those associated with the variations in the previous period, an equation was estimated using data from 1948 through 1963. This appears as equation (3) in table A-1. The coefficients derived from equation (3) were used to predict the injury rate changes in 1963 through 1964. As shown in table A-2, there is no significant difference between the predicted and actual changes. This demonstrates that the increased injury rates in 1964 through 1970 were largely a continuation of old patterns and not the result of new circumstances.

As a further test of stability through time, an analysis of covariance was conducted on the data. The relationship was estimated for years 1948 to 1970 with a dummy variable for 1964 to 1970 and separately for years 1948 to 1963 and 1964 to 1970. The results indicate no significant differences between these formulations and the relationships based on the 1948 to 1970 data without the dummy variable. This implies there is no significant difference between the periods 1948 to 1963 and 1964 to 1970 in either the relationship between dependent and independent variables or the level of the data. The results are summarized in table A-3.

Table A-1

INJURY RATE CHANGE ESTIMATES

(dependent variable: injury frequency rate change)

Estimated Coefficients of Independent Variables (with F values)

	Time Period and Sample Size	Accession Rate Change	Change in Percent of Employees 18–35 Years Old	R^2	D-W	Standard Error	Over-all F
(1)	1948–70 $n = 22$	0.94 (14.39)[a]		0.41	1.38	.67	14.39[a]
(2)	1948–70 $n = 22$	0.73 (9.62)[a]	0.47 (6.42)[b]	0.53	1.97	.60	12.26[a]
(3)	1948–63 $n = 15$	0.95 (9.45)[a]	0.30 (1.49)	0.55	2.00	.68	8.94[a]

[a] Significant at 1 percent confidence level.
[b] Significant at 5 percent confidence level.

Sources: Injury rates are from U.S. Department of Labor, Bureau of Labor Statistics, *Injury Rates* (Washington, D.C., various years).
Accession rate and age data are from U.S. Department of Labor, Bureau of Labor Statistics, *Handbook of Labor Statistics, 1971* (Washington, D.C., 1971).

Table A-2

PREDICTIONS OF 1964–1970 INJURY RATE CHANGES
BASED ON THE EXPERIENCE OF 1948–1963

Year	Actual Change	Pre-dicted Change	t[a]	Actual Injury Rate in Latter Year	Injury Rate in Latter Year Implied by Predicted Change
1963–64	0.4	0.1	−0.6	12.3	12.0
1964–65	0.5	0.5	—	12.8	12.8
1965–66	0.8	0.9	0.2	13.6	13.7
1966–67	0.4	−0.5	−1.46	14.0	13.1
1967–68	0.0	0.4	0.7	14.0	14.4
1968–69	0.8	0.3	−0.8	14.8	14.3
1969–70	0.4	−0.1	−0.8	15.2	14.7

[a] t = (predicted change–actual change)/standard error of prediction. All ts are insignificant at even the 10 percent confidence level.
Source: Predictions based on equation (3) from Table A-1.

Table A-3

ANALYSIS OF COVARIANCE ON
INJURY RATE CHANGE EQUATIONS

Test	Observed F	Critical F (5%)
Differential intercepts	0.78	4.41
Differential slopes	0.80	3.63
Overall homogeneity	0.78	3.24

APPENDIX B

A Statistical Comparison of the Fault and Strict Liability Systems

This appendix describes the statistical analysis which led to the conclusion stated in chapter 3, that a lower level of industrial risk was associated with workers' compensation (shared strict liability) than with a tort system based on determinations of negligence.

An important standard for evaluating the impact of negligence and strict liability on the allocation of resources is the level of risk that prevails under each system. No data are available to measure directly the full amount of such risks consistently through time and across states. However, data on the number of accidental deaths are available starting in 1900. Although these data include non-industrial accidents, certain categories of deaths usually arise from industrial causes. Thus, they can serve as a proxy for industrial deaths and, in turn, as a proxy for industrial risk. As early as 1900, the U.S. Bureau of the Census collected data on accidental deaths as part of their *Vital Statistics* series.[1] The data are categorized by cause; however, many of the definitions have changed over the years. After examining the definitions, it was determined that the only consistent series of data reflecting industrial risks through the relevant period were those deaths caused by machinery accidents (other than motor vehicle accidents).[2] According to a 1935 report of the Bureau of the Census, such accidents caused approximately 16 percent of industrial deaths. More important for

---

This appendix is a summary of the statistical section in James R. Chelius, "Liability for Industrial Accidents: A Comparison of Negligence and Strict Liability Systems," *Journal of Legal Studies*, vol. 5, no. 2 (June 1976), pp. 293-309.

[1] The data were collected in those states which participated in the Bureau of the Census program by using standardized death certificates and uniform cause of death definitions. The definitions are included in U.S. Department of Commerce, Bureau of the Census, *Manual of the International List of Causes of Death, 1902* (Washington, D.C., 1902) and the 1909, 1920, 1929, and 1939 revisions of this manual. Data are from U.S. Department of Commerce, Bureau of the Census, *Mortality Statistics* (Washington, D.C., various years).

[2] Not all states had data for all years. The states in the sample were Connecticut, Virginia, Vermont, New Hampshire, Wisconsin, South Carolina, Massachusetts, Michigan, New York, New Jersey, Minnesota, Washington, Rhode Island, Missouri, Ohio, Indiana, Colorado, California, Florida, Utah, Maine, Kentucky, North Carolina, Montana, Pennsylvania, and Maryland.

purposes of this analysis is the fact that approximately 87 percent of such machinery deaths occurred in workplaces.[3] Several other potentially useful proxies for industrial risks had to be eliminated. Traumatisms by "cutting or piercing instruments" as well as traumatisms by "fall, crushing or landslide" did not have consistent definitions over a long period. Data on deaths caused by electricity were not collected until 1910, and thus would not be available for many states in the pre-workers'-compensation period. Deaths in mines and quarries were not used because of the substantial variations in the number of such industries among the states.

In order to allow for variations in the number of deaths due to the number of people exposed, the data were formulated as the number of deaths per number of people employed.[4] Before the relationship between the machinery death rate and liability arrangement can be examined, several other factors that potentially could influence the death rate must be considered. For instance, over the period of analysis (1900-1940), there were changes in per capita exposure to machinery, the business cycle, and the technology of medical care. Factors like these can be taken into account by formulating the measure of risk as a ratio of the experience of a particular state for a particular year relative to the average experience in that year for the country as a whole. Thus, factors such as medical technology, which could be expected to influence death rates but which are not likely to have a differential impact on individual states, need not be directly considered.

Safety regulation other than liability arrangements might also influence the level of risk in workplaces. Such regulation took the form of direct controls over industrial safety practices, for example, requiring use of sturdy ladders and guard railings. To account for this possibility, the control system of each sample state was examined for the years in the analysis. Since safety regulation was a significant governmental concern in this period, particularly in the earlier years, the status of each state's regulatory effort was well documented by publications of the United States Department of Commerce and Labor.[5] But it was apparent that any attempt to make subtle quantitative distinctions between them was futile. It was decided, therefore, to characterize these regulations simply by the absence or presence of a fairly substantial regulatory effort. The operating definition of this obviously subjective criterion was the presence of a control effort that involved more than just the passage of a law prohibiting unsafe practices. By this criterion a state had to have funds budgeted for the enforcement of the law as well as some enforcement mechanism.

[3] U.S. Department of Commerce, Bureau of the Census, *Vital Statistics*, vol. 3 (Washington, D.C., 1935), p. 107. U.S. Department of Commerce, Bureau of the Census, *Vital Statistics–Special Reports*, vol. 3 (Washington, D.C., 1935), p. 107. The data are for the year 1935 only.

[4] No state/year data on the number of people employed are directly available. These data were estimated using labor force figures for each census year, with intercensus years derived by interpolation. Each of the state/year figures was then multiplied by the percentage of the labor force that was employed in that year. Data are from U.S. Department of Commerce, Bureau of the Census, *Census of the U.S., Population* (Washington, D.C., various years).

[5] A complete list of these publications is contained in Chelius, "Liability for Industrial Accidents," pp. 307-09.

The basic model to be estimated is:

$$D_{ij}/D_{US,j} = \alpha_0 + \alpha_1 (EL) + \alpha_2 (WC) + \alpha_3 (\text{Controls}) + \mu$$

where:

$D_{ij}/D_{US,j} =$ the ratio of the machinery death rate in state i in year j to the machinery death rate for the U.S. in year j.

$EL =$ a dummy variable representing the presence of an employer's-liability law lagged one year.

$WC =$ a dummy variable representing the presence of a workers'-compensation law lagged one year.

Controls $=$ a dummy variable representing the presence of a regulatory system using enforceable safety standards lagged one year.

$\mu =$ error term.

The independent variables were lagged one year to allow for the varying time within the year that laws went into effect as well as the fact that the impact of a change would not be instantaneous. In using dummy variables for employer's liability and workers' compensation, the coefficients α_1 and α_2 are interpreted as the impact of these laws on the death rate relative to the impact of the common law. Similarly, the coefficient α_3 measures the impact of safety-standard regulation relative to the absence of such regulation.

Since the sample combines time-series and cross-section data, it is necessary to test the model for appropriate specification. Three possibilities were examined. First, the relationship between the independent and dependent variables could be homogeneous over time and across states, thus implying a model which pools years and states with no distinction. Second, the independent variables could have the same impact on the dependent variable in each state but with the level of the dependent variable being substantially different in each state, thus implying a pooling of years and states with a dummy variable (separate intercept) for each state. Finally the relationship could be different in each state, implying a separate regression equation for each state. A covariance analysis which compared the residual variance for each of these specifications indicated that it is inappropriate to pool the states and years without allowing for interstate differences in death rates. This analysis demonstrates that the relationship between the independent and dependent variables is sufficiently similar across states that it is unnecessary to estimate a regression equation for each state. The death rate ratios are, therefore, different in various states but the coefficients of the independent variables are similar in each state. Such a situation dictates that the model be estimated using a dummy variable for each of the sample states. The coefficient of each of these state dummies represents the impact of the characteristics in each state that cause the state's death rate to be at a particular level.[6]

The results of estimating the equation using ordinary least-squares regression were that both employer's liability and workers' compensation laws were associated with significantly lower death rates. The safety-

---

[6] For a discussion of this issue, see J. Johnston, *Econometric Methods*, 2nd ed. (New York: McGraw-Hill, 1972), pp. 192-207.

controls regulation was not associated with any significant change in the death rate. The results of the estimation of this model are presented in table B-1, equation 1.

An estimation of the equation which distinguished compulsory and elective workers'-compensation systems was also calculated. The results indicated that both types of workers' compensation were associated with relatively lower death rates. The regression coefficients indicated that elective laws were associated with a larger reduction in relative death rates.[7]

The equation was also estimated using measures of the age and percentage of women of each state's labor force. This was done to determine if these factors had changed within the state so as to influence the results. Other research has found that age and sex characteristics are associated with the rate of accidents. Each variable was formulated as the ratio of a state's characteristics to the characteristics for the United States. Although age and sex variables had the anticipated signs (age positive and percentage of women negative) neither variable was significant.[8]

One factor that could invalidate the results is the nature of technological change between 1900 and 1940. If the twenty-six sample states had coincidently developed a safer technology than was used by the average state, the safety benefits of the changes would be inappropriately assigned to changes in liability systems. This possibility was investigated by alternatively restricting the sample to the years 1900–1920, 1900–1925, and 1900–1930 (table B-1, equations 2, 3, and 4). Restricting the sample in this manner allows less time for technological change than the full period of 1900 to 1940. The results using each of the restricted samples confirm the results of the full sample—employer's liability and workers' compensation were associated with lower death rates, but the safety standards regulation had no impact.

In order to focus more specifically on the changeover from negligence to strict liability, an analysis of the periods immediately before and after the change was also conducted. The average machine death rate for the five-year period before and the five-year period after the change to workmen's compensation was analyzed using a dummy variable to represent the difference in liability arrangements. Since some states had differing mixtures of common law and employer's liability in the pre-workmen's com-

---

[7] The coefficient for elective workmen's compensation was —0.8 with a t value of 7.5. For compulsory laws, the coefficient was —0.7 with a t value of 4.4. In states with elective laws, states usually had provisions that eliminated the common law defenses for employers who choose not to be covered by the statute. If an employee elected not to be covered by the law the employer typically retained the traditional common law defenses.

[8] The age variable used was the average age of population for those aged 15 to 64. The sex variable was the percentage of women in the labor force. Each variable was available by state for census years only; the intercensus years were obtained by interpolation. Based on the literature of occupational safety, it was anticipated that a higher percentage of women would be associated with a lower death rate. The literature also indicates that older workers are subject to more severe injuries, hence it was anticipated that higher average ages would be associated with a greater death rate. Data are from *Census of the U.S., Population*, various years.

Table B-1
IMPACT OF LIABILITY CHANGES ON DEATH RATES ($D_{ij}/D_{US,j}$) AS MEASURED BY COEFFICIENTS OF EMPLOYER'S LIABILITY (*EL*) AND WORKERS' COMPENSATION (*WC*)

	Coefficients and *t* Values Associated with the Independent Variables		

(1)	*EL*	*WC*	*Controls*
	—0.6[a]	—1.4[a]	+0.6
	(—4.0)	(—14.0)	(1.7)

$R^2 = .29$, $F = 12.9$[a], $n = 907$
Estimated using available data, 1900–1940

(2)	*EL*	*WC*	*Controls*
	—0.8[a]	—1.4[a]	+0.6
	(—3.8)	(—10.8)	(1.3)

$R^2 = .53$, $F = 8.3$[a], $n = 621$
Estimated using available data, 1900–1930

(3)	*EL*	*WC*	*Controls*
	—0.8[a]	—1.4[a]	+0.7
	(—3.5)	(—8.8)	(1.3)

$R^2 = .51$, $F = 5.9$[a], $n = 491$
Estimated using available data, 1900–1925

(4)	*EL*	*WC*	*Controls*
	—1.0[a]	—1.5[a]	+0.7
	(—3.0)	(—6.4)	(1.0)

$R^2 = .50$, $F = 9.0$[a], $n = 361$
Estimated using available data, 1900–1920

[a] Significant at the 1 percent level. All equations were estimated using dummy variables for each state except Connecticut as dictated by the covariance analysis. The coefficients for these dummy variables and the constant term are not presented.

pensation period, the analysis combines these forms into a general negligence category without distinguishing between them. The coefficient on *WC* thus represents the impact of workers' compensation compared with negligence liability. As shown in table B-2, the analysis indicates that death rates were significantly lower under the strict liability system. A similar result was obtained when three-year averages were used.

Table B-2
IMPACT OF LIABILITY CHANGES ON DEATH RATES $(D_{ij}/D_{US,j})$ AS MEASURED BY THE WORKERS' COMPENSATION COEFFICIENT (WC)

3 Year Pre/Post Averages	5 Year Pre/Post Averages
WC	WC
-0.19[a]	-0.32[a]
(-3.7)	(-4.8)
$R^2 = 0.96, F = 11.26$[a]$, n = 52$	$R^2 = 0.91, F = 4.7$[a]$, n = 42$

[a] Significant at the 1 percent level.

Note: The regression framework used in this analysis is equivalent to the single-factor, repeated-measures analysis of variance design. Numbers in parentheses are t values. Both equations were estimated using dummy variables for each state except Connecticut as dictated by the covariance analysis. The coefficients for these dummy variables and the constant term are not presented.

APPENDIX C

Statistical Evidence on the Impact
of Benefit Levels

In chapter 3, it was noted that empirical analysis implies that higher levels of workers' compensation benefits are associated with a higher rate of occupational injuries. This appendix presents the statistical analysis yielding this conclusion.

It is hypothesized that the following equation represents the relationship between the observed injury rate and independent factors:

(1) INJURY RATE $= b_{11} + b_{12}(AGE) + b_{13}(SEX) + b_{14}(HOURS) + b_{15}(HIRES) + b_{16}(SIZE) + b_{17}(W\hat{A}GE) + b_{18}(INDUSTRY) + b_{19}(WC) + \mu,$

where:[1]

INJURY RATE $=$ the number of disabling injuries per million man-hours of exposure.

AGE $=$ the average age of the industry's work force in each state. Studies have found that younger workers have more accidents.

SEX $=$ the percentage of women in the industry's work force in each state. Studies have found that women have fewer accidents than men.

HOURS $=$ the average number of hours worked per week in the the industry in each state. This variable is a proxy for the impact of work pace and fatigue in producing injuries.

This appendix is a summary of James Robert Chelius, "An Empirical Test of the Coase Theorem," working paper, Krannert School of Management, Purdue University, West Lafayette, Indiana.

[1] The data sources used were: U.S. Department of Labor, Bureau of Labor Statistics, *Injury Rates, 1966 and 1967*, Bulletin No. 360 (Washington, D.C., 1969); Unpublished files, Office of Research and Statistics, Social Security Administration, U.S. Department of Health, Education, and Welfare were used for age and sex data; U.S. Department of Labor, Bureau of Labor Statistics, *Employment and Earnings, States and Areas, 1939-69*, Bulletin 1370-7 was used for hours and wages data; U.S. Department of Labor, Bureau of Labor Statistics, *Handbook of Labor Statistics, 1970*, Bulletin 1666 was used for new hires data; unpublished files, American Insurance Association, New York, New York, were used for the workers' compensation data.

HIRES = the new hires rate for the industry. Since inexperienced workers incur a disproportionate share of work injuries, this variable serves as a proxy for the number of inexperienced workers.

SIZE = the average number of employees per establishment for each industry in each state. There appear to be economies of scale in accident and disease prevention, and this variable serves as a proxy for this phenomenon.

WÂGE = the average wage rate for each industry in each state as estimated in equation (2). This represents human capital embodied in each worker. It is expected that the higher the level of this capital, the more effort will be devoted to protecting it. However, the injury rate is potentially one of the determinants of the wage rate in that, *ceteris paribus*, a higher risk of injury will induce a higher wage to compensate for that risk. This simultaneity gives rise to the need for the two-equation model with the wage and injury rates as endogenous variables.

INDUSTRY = a dummy variable for each industry except foods. Covariance analysis indicates that each industry has a different injury rate level but that the impact of the independent variables on the dependent variable is approximately the same in all industries. This implies a similar regression coefficient but a different intercept for each industry. Thus, a dummy variable for each industry is the most appropriate construction of the relationships.

WC = an actuarial measure of worker's compensation benefits for each state. This reflects variations in the percentage of employee-injury costs for which the employer is liable without regard to fault.

μ = error term.

The wage equation includes the injury rate as an endogenous variable.

$$(2) \quad \text{WAGES} = b_{21} + b_{22}(\text{HRS}) + b_{23}(\text{SEX}) + b_{24}(\text{EDUC}) + b_{25}(\text{UNION}) + b_{26}(\text{AGE}) + b_{27}(\text{RACE}) + b_{28}(\text{SOUTH}) + b_{29}(\text{WC}) + b_{2,10}(\text{INJURY RATE}) + \mu_2$$

where the variables are defined as above with the following additions:[2]

EDUC = median school years completed, by industry, a measure of general human capital, 1970.

UNION = the percentage of workers in establishments with a majority of workers under a collective-bargaining agreement, by industry, by region, in 1958 (stability in these percentages makes use of 1958 data acceptable; this is the latest year for which subnational unionization data are available).

RACE = percentage of nonwhites by industry, by state, 1970.

SOUTH = a dummy variable equaling 1 for southern states and 0 for all others. Observations included all available 2-digit Standard Industrial Classification industry averages from eighteen sample states.

The regression estimation yields the conclusion that the injury rate varies with the extent of liability on employers. Higher levels of benefits are found to be associated with higher injury rates. Although no evidence

---

[2] The data sources used were: U.S. Department of Commerce, Bureau of the Census, U.S. Census of Population: *Characteristics of the Population* (1970), table 184 for race data and *Industrial Characteristics*, table 1 for education data; H. M. Douty, "Collective Bargaining Coverage in Factory Employment, 1958," *Monthly Labor Review* (April 1960), pp. 345-49.

was found that wage premiums reflect the degree of risk, most of the factors used to isolate the impact of the liability arrangements performed as expected. The results are presented in table C-1.

It is useful to consider alternative explanations that could account for this result. One possibility is that public officials in states with high injury rates enact higher workmen's compensation benefits and that as a result higher injury rates cause a greater degree of employer liability. To account for such a possibility the empirical model was reestimated with benefits as an endogenous variable. The results, however, are essentially the same as with workers' compensation as an exogenous variable.

It is also possible that the results derive from increased *reporting* of injuries rather than an increased real number of injuries, although the data used are independent of the workers' compensation system. Workers might find the higher benefits an inducement to report injuries that would otherwise go unreported. It may also be that higher workers'-compensation benefits decrease the cost of an accident to risk-averse workers by replacing an uncertain income stream with a stable income stream. Thus, more injuries occur because cost of injuries to the workers is reduced.

Table C-1

ESTIMATED RELATIONSHIPS BETWEEN INJURY RATE, WAGE, AND INDEPENDENT VARIABLES

Injury Rate $= -3.09 + 0.10$ AGE -0.30 SEX
$\quad\quad\quad\quad$ (0.15) $\quad$ (0.88) $\quad\quad\quad$ (4.20)

$\quad\quad\quad\quad +1.00$ HRS $+ 2.20$ HIRES
$\quad\quad\quad\quad$ (2.07) $\quad\quad\quad$ (2.00)

$\quad\quad\quad\quad -0.03$ SIZE -0.21 WÂGE
$\quad\quad\quad\quad$ (3.86) $\quad\quad\quad$ (2.80)

$\quad\quad\quad\quad +0.08$ WC
$\quad\quad\quad\quad$ (2.15)

$\quad\quad\quad\quad R^2 = 0.43$ SEE 83.1

Wage $= -4.69 + 1.97$ HRS -0.63 SEX
$\quad\quad\quad$ (1.17) $\quad$ (2.27) $\quad\quad\quad$ (5.83)

$\quad\quad\quad\quad +11.21$ EDUC $+ 0.003$ UNION
$\quad\quad\quad\quad$ (4.13) $\quad\quad\quad\quad$ (0.04)

$\quad\quad\quad\quad -0.52$ AGE -0.05 RACE -12.5 SOUTH
$\quad\quad\quad\quad$ (2.16) $\quad\quad\quad$ (0.39) $\quad\quad\quad\quad$ (2.60)

$\quad\quad\quad\quad +0.15$ WC -1.15 INJURY RATE
$\quad\quad\quad\quad$ (2.33) $\quad\quad\quad$ (4.19)

$\quad\quad\quad\quad R^2 = 0.68$ SEE 264.8

Note: Numbers in parentheses are the ratio or the coefficients to standard errors. Standard significance tests do not strictly apply under this two-stage estimating procedure.

APPENDIX D
Details of the Suggested Reforms

This appendix presents key features of the proposed reforms of the workers' compensation system.[1] The first section presents the recommendations of the National Commission on State Workmen's Compensation Laws. The highlights of the National Workers' Compensation Act of 1975 are given in the second section.

The Recommendations of the National Commission

The National Commission issued eighty-four recommendations in its 1972 *Report*. Nineteen of these recommendations were deemed to be "the essential elements of a modern workmen's compensation program." The commission urged "that compliance of the States with these essential recommendations be evaluated on July 1, 1975, and that, if necessary, Congress with no further delay in the effective date should guarantee compliance with these recommendations."[2] As of that date the states had, on average, complied with 12.8 of the nineteen recommendations. As of January 1, 1976, the states averaged compliance with 13.2 of the nineteen.[3]

The essential recommendations are:[4]

(1) We recommend that coverage by workmen's compensation laws be compulsory and that no waivers be permitted. (R2.1) [48 states, compulsory coverage; 41 states, no waivers]

---

[1] Chapter 4 analyzes these proposals.

[2] *The Report of the National Commission on State Workmen's Compensation Laws* (Washington, D.C., 1972), p. 26.

[3] Calculations are based on data from "Substantial Compliance of State Laws with Workers' Compensation Recommended Standards," 1st ed. and supplement, the "Report of the Substantial Compliance Subcommittee of the Ad Hoc Committee to Consider State Compliance with Workers' Compensation Recommended Standards" (Washington, D.C.: Workers' Disability Income Systems Inc., 1976).

[4] The numbers in parentheses refer to the numbering system used in the *Report*. The number before the period refers to the chapter which contains the recommendation. The number after the period is the sequence number of the recommendation within the chapter. Items in brackets refer to the number of states that substantially met the requirements of the recommendation as of January 1, 1976. Source: *Substantial Compliance Report*, 1st supplement.

(2) We recommend that employers not be exempted from workmen's compensation coverage because of the number of their employees. (R2.2) [46 states]

(3) We recommend a two-stage approach to the coverage of farmworkers. First, we recommend that as of July 1, 1973, each agriculture employer who has an annual payroll that in total exceeds $1,000 be required to provide workmen's compensation coverage to all of his employees. As a second stage, we recommend that, as of July 1, 1975, farmworkers be covered on the same basis as all other employees. (R2.4) [21 states]

(4) We recommend that as of July 1, 1975, household workers and all casual workers be covered under workmen's compensation at least to the extent they are covered by Social Security. (R2.5) [4 states]

(5) We recommend that workmen's compensation coverage be mandatory for all government employees. (R2.6) [44 states]

(6) We recommend that there be no exemptions for any class of employees, such as professional athletes or employees of charitable organizations. (R2.7) [38 states]

(7) We recommend that an employee or his survivor be given the choice of filing a workmen's compensation claim in the State where the injury or death occurred, or where the employment was principally localized, or where the employee was hired. (R2.11) [28 states]

(8) We recommend that all States provide full coverage for work-related diseases. (R2.13) [48 states]

(9) We recommend there be no statutory limits of time or dollar amount for medical care or physical rehabilitation services for any work-related impairment. (R4.2) [47 states]

(10) We recommend that the right to medical and physical rehabilitation benefits not terminate by the mere passage of time. (R4.4) [42 states]

(11) [As a transitional formula to the 80 percent of spendable earnings standard] we recommend that, subject to the State's maximum weekly benefit, temporary total-disability benefits be at least 66⅔ percent of the worker's gross weekly wage. (R3.7) [49 states]

(12) We recommend that as of July 1, 1973, the maximum weekly benefit for temporary total disability be at least 66⅔ percent of the State's average weekly wage, and that as of July 1, 1975, the maximum be at least 100 percent of the State's average weekly wage. (R3.8) [22 states]

(13) We recommend that the definition of permanent total disability used in most States be retained. However, in those few States which permit the payment of permanent total disability benefits to workers who retain substantial earning capacity, we recommend that our benefit proposals be applicable only to those cases which meet the test of permanent total disability used in most States. (R3.11) [50 states]

(14) We recommend that, subject to the State's maximum weekly benefit, permanent total disability benefits be at least 66⅔ percent of the worker's gross weekly wage. (R3.12) [48 states]

(15) We recommend that as of July 1, 1973, the maximum weekly benefit for permanent total disability be at least 66⅔ percent of the State's

weekly wage, and that as of July 1, 1975, the maximum be at least 100 percent of the State's average weekly wage. (R3.15) [20 states]

(16) [As a transitional formula to the 80 percent of spendable earnings standard] we recommend that, subject to the State's maximum weekly benefit, death benefits be at least 66⅔ percent of the worker's gross weekly wage. (R3.21) [39 states]

(17) We recommend that as of July 1, 1973, the maximum weekly death benefit be at least 66⅔ percent of the State's average weekly wage, and that as of July 1, 1975, the maximum be at least 100 percent of the State's average weekly wage. (R3.23) [16 states]

(18) We recommend that total disability benefits be paid for the duration of the worker's disability, or for life, without any limitations as to dollar amount or time. (R3.17) [41 states]

(19) We recommend that death benefits be paid to a widow or widower for life or until remarriage, and in the event of remarriage we recommend that two years' benefit be paid in a lump sum to the widow or widower. We also recommend that benefits for a dependent child be continued at least until the child reaches 18, or beyond such age if actually dependent, or at least until age 25 if enrolled as a full-time student in any accredited educational institution. (R3.25) [29 states, duration spouse; 24 states, remarriage dowry; 29 states, duration child; 20 states, duration student]

The following are the recommendations which the commission felt to be desirable but not essential:

(20) We recommend that workmen's compensation coverage be extended to all occupations and industries, without regard to the degree of hazard of the occupation or industry. (R2.3)

(21) We recommend that the term "employee" be defined as broadly as possible. (R2.8)

(22) We recommend that workmen's compensation be made available on an optional basis for employers, partners, and self-employed persons. (R2.9)

(23) We recommend that workers be eligible for workmen's compensation benefits from the first moment of their employment. (R2.10)

(24) We recommend that the "accident" requirement be dropped as a test for compensability. (R2.12)

(25) We recommend that the "arising out of and in the course of the employment" test be used to determine coverage of injuries and diseases. (R2.14)

(26) We recommend that the etiology of a disease, being a medical question, be determined by a disability evaluation unit under the control and supervision of the workmen's compensation agency. (R2.15)

(27) We further recommend that for deaths and impairments apparently caused by a combination of work-related and non-work-related sources, issues of causation be determined by the disability evaluation unit. (R2.16)

(28) We recommend that full workmen's compensation benefits be paid for an impairment or death resulting from both work-related and nonwork-related causes if the work-related factor was significant cause of the impairment or death. (R2.17)

(29) We recommend that workmen's compensation benefits be the exclusive liability of an employer when an employee is impaired or dies because of a work-related injury or disease. (R2.18)

(30) We recommend that suits by employees against negligent third parties generally be permitted. Immunity from negligence actions should be extended to any third party performing the normal functions of the employer. (R2.19)

(31) We recommend that, subject to the State's maximum weekly benefit, a worker's weekly benefit be at least 80 percent of his spendable weekly earnings. (R3.1)

(32) [As a transitional formula to the 80 percent of spendable earnings standard] we recommend that, subject to the State's maximum weekly benefit, a worker's weekly benefit be at least 66⅔ percent of his gross weekly wage. (R3.2)

(33) We recommend that, if our recommended benefit increases for workmen's compensation are adopted, the benefits of other public insurance programs should be coordinated with workmen's compensation benefits. In general, workmen's compensation should be the primary source of benefits for work-related injuries and diseases. (R3.3)

(34) We recommend that workmen's compensation benefits not be reduced by the amount of any payments from a welfare program or other program based on need. (R3.4)

(35) We recommend that the waiting period for benefits be no more than three days and that a period of no more than 14 days be required to qualify for retroactive benefits for days lost. (R3.5)

(36) We recommend that, subject to the State's maximum weekly benefit, temporary total disability benefits be at least 80 percent of the worker's spendable weekly earnings. This formula should be used as soon as feasible or, in any case, as soon as the maximum weekly benefit in a State exceeds 100 percent of the State's average weekly wage. (R3.6)

(37) We recommend that as of July 1, 1977, the maximum weekly benefit for temporary total disability be at least 133⅓ percent of the State's average weekly wage; as of July 1, 1979, the maximum should be at least 166⅔ percent of the State's average weekly wage, and on and after July 1, 1981, the maximum should be at least 200 percent of the State's average weekly wage. (R3.9)

(38) We recommend that, for all maximum weekly benefits, the maximum be linked to the State's average weekly wage for the latest available year as determined by the agency administering the State employment security program. (R3.10)

(39) We recommend that, subject to the State's maximum weekly benefit, permanent total disability benefits be at least 80 percent of the worker's spendable weekly earnings. This formula should be used as

soon as feasible or, in any case, as soon as the maximum weekly benefit in the State exceeds 100 percent of the State's average weekly wage. (R3.13)

(40) We recommend that beneficiaries in permanent total disability cases have their benefits increased through time in the same proportion as increases in the State's average weekly wage. (R3.14)

(41) We recommend that as of July 1, 1977, the maximum weekly benefit for permanent total disability be at least 133⅓ percent of the State's average weekly wage; as of July 1, 1979, the maximum should be at least 166⅔ percent of the State's average weekly wage; and on and after July 1, 1981, the maximum should be at least 200 percent of the State's average weekly wage. (R3.16)

(42) We recommend that, provided our other recommendations for permanent total disability benefits are adopted by the States, the Disability Insurance program of Social Security continue to reduce payments for those workers receiving workmen's compensation benefits. (R3.18)

(43) We recommend that each State undertake a thorough examination of permanent partial benefits and that the Federal Government sponsor a comprehensive review of present and potential approaches to permanent partial benefits. (R3.19)

(44) We recommend that, subject to the State's maximum weekly benefit, death benefits be at least 80 percent of the worker's spendable weekly earnings. This formula should be used as soon as feasible or, in any case, as soon as the maximum weekly benefit in a State exceeds 100 percent of the State's average weekly wage. (R3.20)

(45) We recommend that beneficiaries in death cases have their benefits increased through time in the same proportion as increases in the State's average weekly wage. (R3.22)

(46) We recommend that as of July 1, 1977, the maximum weekly death benefit be at least 133⅓ percent of the State's average weekly wage; as of July 1, 1979, the maximum should be at least 166⅔ percent of the State's average weekly wage, and on and after July 1, 1981, the maximum should be at least 200 percent of the State's average weekly wage. (R3.24)

(47) We recommend that the minimum weekly benefit for death cases be at least 50 percent of the State's average weekly wage. (R3.26)

(48) We recommend that workmen's compensation death benefits be reduced by the amount of any payments received from Social Security by the deceased worker's family. (R3.27)

(49) We recommend that the worker be permitted the initial selection of his physician, either from among all licensed physicians in the State or from a panel of physicians selected or approved by the workmen's compensation agency. (R4.1)

(50) We recommend that the workmen's compensation agency have discretion to determine the appropriate medical and rehabilitation services in each case. There should be no arbitrary limits by regulation or

statute on the types of medical service or licensed health care facilities which can be authorized by the agency. (R4.3)

(51) We recommend that each workmen's compensation agency establish a medical-rehabilitation division, with authority to effectively supervise medical care and rehabilitation services. (R4.5)

(52) We recommend that every employer or carrier acting as employer's agent be required to cooperate with the medical-rehabilitation division in every instance when an employee may need rehabilitation services. (R4.6)

(53) We recommend that the medical-rehabilitation division be given the specific responsibility of assuring that every worker who could benefit from vocational rehabilitation services be offered those services. (R4.7)

(54) We also recommend that the employer pay all costs of vocational rehabilitation necessary to return a worker to suitable employment and authorized by the workmen's compensation agency. (R4.8)

(55) We recommend that the workmen's compensation agency be authorized to provide special maintenance benefits for a worker during the period of his rehabilitation. The maintenance benefits would be in addition to the worker's other benefits. (R4.9)

(56) We recommend that each State establish a second-injury fund with broad coverage of pre-existing impairments. (R4.10)

(57) We recommend that the second-injury fund be financed by charges against all carriers, State funds, and self-insuring employers in proportion to the benefits paid by each, or by appropriations from general revenue, or by both sources. (R4.11)

(58) We recommend that workmen's compensation agencies publicize second-injury funds to employees and employers and interpret eligibility requirements for the funds liberally in order to encourage employment of the physically handicapped. (R4.12)

(59) We recommend that a standard workmen's compensation reporting system be devised which will mesh with the forms required by the Occupational Safety and Health Act of 1970 and permit the exchange of information among Federal and State safety agencies and State workmen's compensation agencies. (R5.1)

(60) We recommend that insurance carriers be required to provide loss prevention services and that the workmen's compensation agency carefully audit the services. The agency should insure that all carriers doing business in the State furnish effective loss prevention services to all employers and, in particular, should determine that reasonable efforts are devoted to safety programs for smaller firms. State-operated workmen's compensation funds should provide similar accident prevention services under independent audit procedures, where practicable. Self-insuring employers should likewise be subject to audit with respect to the adequacy of their safety programs. (R5.2)

(61) We recommend that, subject to sound actuarial standards, the experience rating principle be extended to as many employers as practicable. (R5.3)

(62) We recommend that, subject to sound actuarial standards, the relationship between an employer's favorable experience relative to the experience of other employers in its insurance classification be more equitably reflected in the employer's insurance charges. (R5.4)

(63) We recommend that each State utilize a workmen's compensation agency to fulfill the administrative obligations of a modern workmen's compensation program. (R6.1)

(64) We recommend that in those States where the chief administrator is a member of the appeals board, the Governor have the authority to select which member of the appeals board or commission will be the chief administrator. In those States where the administrator is not a member of the appeals board or commission, his term of office should either be indefinite (where he serves at the pleasure of the Governor) or be for a limited term, short enough to insure that a Governor will, sometime during his term of office, have the opportunity to select the chief administrator. (R6.2)

(65) We recommend that the members of the appeals board or commission be appointed for substantial terms. (R6.3)

(66) We also recommend that agency employees be given civil service status or similar protection. (R6.4)

(67) We recommend that the members of the appeals board or commission and the chief administrator be selected by the Governor subject to confirmation by the legislature or other confirming body. The other employees of the agency should be appointed by the chief administrator or selected in accordance with the State's civil service procedure. Insofar as practical, all employees of the agency should be full-time, with no outside employment. Salaries should be commensurate with this full-time status. (R6.5)

(68) We recommend that an advisory committee in each State conduct a thorough examination of the State's workmen's compensation law in the light of our Report. (R6.6)

(69) We recommend that the workmen's compensation agency be adequately financed by an assessment on insurance premiums or benefits paid plus an equivalent assessment against self-insurers. (R6.7)

(70) We recommend that the workmen's compensation agency develop a continuing program to inform employees and employers about the salient features of the State's workmen's compensation program. (R6.8)

(71) We recommend that the employee or his surviving dependents be required to give notice as soon as practical to the employer concerning the work-related impairment or death. This notice requirement would be met if the employer or his agent, such as an insurance carrier, has actual knowledge of the impairment or death, or if oral or written notice is given to the employer. (R6.9)

(72) We recommend that employers be required to report to the agency all work-related injuries or diseases which result in death, in time lost beyond the shift or working day in which the impairment affects the worker, or in permanent impairment to the worker. (R6.10)

(73) We recommend that, for those injuries and diseases which must be reported to the workmen's compensation agency, the period allowed for employees to file claims not begin to run until the employer's notice of the work-related impairment or death is filed with the workmen's compensation agency. (R6.11)

(74) We recommend that the administrator of the workmen's compensation agency have discretion under his rulemaking authority to decide which reports are needed in uncontested cases. (R6.12)

(75) We recommend that the time limit for initiating a claim be three years after the date the claimant knows or, by exercise of reasonable diligence should have known, of the existence of the impairment and its possible relationship to his employment, or within three years after the employee first experiences a loss of wages which the employee knows or, by exercise of reasonable diligence should have known, was because of the work-related impairment. If benefits have previously been provided, the claim period should begin on the date benefits were last furnished. (R6.13)

(76) We recommend that where there is an appellate level within the workmen's compensation agency, the decisions of the workmen's compensation agency be reviewed by the courts only on questions of law. (R6.14)

(77) We recommend that attorneys' fees for all parties be reported for each case, and that the fees be regulated under the rule making authority of the workmen's compensation administrator. (R6.15)

(78) We recommend that the workmen's compensation agency permit compromise and release agreements only rarely and only after a conference or hearing before the workmen's compensation agency and approval by the agency. (R6.16)

(79) We recommend that the agency be particularly reluctant to permit compromise and release agreements which terminate medical and rehabilitation benefits. (R6.17)

(80) We also recommend that lump-sum payments, even in the absence of a compromise and release agreement, be permitted only with agency approval. (R6.18)

(81) We recommend that the administrator have the authority to prescribe the reports which must be submitted by employers, employees, attorneys, doctors, carriers, and other parties involved in the workmen's compensation delivery system. (R6.19)

(82) We recommend that the States be free to continue their present insurance arrangements or to permit private insurance, self-insurance, and State funds where any of these types of insurance are now excluded. (R6.20)

(83) We recommend that procedures be established in each State to provide benefits to employees whose benefits are endangered because of an insolvent carrier or employer or because an employer fails to comply with the law mandating the purchase of workmen's compensation insurance. (R6.21)

(84) We recommend that, because inflation has adversely affected the payments of those claimants whose benefits began when benefits were not at their current levels, a workmen's compensation retroactive benefit fund be established to increase the benefits to current levels for those claimants still entitled to compensation. (R6.22)

The National Workers' Compensation Act of 1975

In June 1975, Senators Williams and Javits introduced on behalf of themselves and Senators Pell, Kennedy, Mondale, Hathaway, and Humphrey, the National Workers' Compensation Act of 1975, Senate Bill 2018. The following are the major sections of the proposed act:

Findings and Declaration of Purpose

SEC. 2. (a) The Congress finds and declares that—

(1) many thousands of American workers are killed or permanently disabled and millions more are incapacitated from injuries and disease arising out of and in the course of their employment;

(2) injuries, diseases, and deaths arising out of and in the course of employment, constitute a burden upon interstate commerce and have a substantial adverse effect upon the general welfare;

(3) work-related injuries and occupational diseases frequently occur during the workers' most productive years which often result in hardship for dependents and families;

(4) the vast majority of these injured and ill workers, and their families, are dependent on State workers' compensation systems for economic security, medical treatment, rehabilitation, and reemployment assistance when they suffer an injury, disease, or death arising out of and in the course of their employment;

(5) American workers who suffer from injuries, diseases, or death arising out of and in the course of their employment, and the national interest, are best served by a comprehensive national workers' compensation system;

(6) existing State workers' compensation laws do not provide a prompt and comprehensive system of compensation for injuries, diseases, or deaths arising out of and in the course of employment;

(7) the basic national objectives for a comprehensive workers' compensation system include (A) universal coverage of employees and work-related injuries and diseases; (B) substantial protection against interruption of income; (C) provision of prompt and adequate medical care and rehabilitation services in order to correct work-related injuries and to restore such injured workers to gainful employment; (D) encouragement of safety; and (E) an effective system for delivery of benefits and services;

(8) that basic, national minimum requirements for State workers' compensation laws must be mandated by the Congress, and that Congress must provide for a national enforcement procedure for the protection of workers who are injured, killed, or who contract diseases, which arise out of and in the course of employment.

(b) It is the purpose of this act through the exercise of the power of Congress to regulate commerce among the several States and with foreign nations, and to provide for the general welfare, to—

(1) establish minimum workers' compensation benefits for employees in the States and to establish administrative requirements for State workers' compensation agencies;

(2) establish appropriate procedures for enforcement of such benefits and requirements through State workers' compensation systems;

(3) encourage and provide technical and financial assistance to the States to make improvements in existing workers' compensation systems so as (A) to provide all workers and their families a uniform, adequate, prompt, and equitable system of workers' compensation in the event they suffer work-related disabling injury, disease, or death; and (B) to restore disabled workers through medical and vocational rehabilitation services to the fullest possible physical, mental, and economic usefulness.

Definitions

SEC. 3. For the purposes of this Act . . .

(3) the term "employer" means any person who employs any individual, but shall not include the United States;

(4) the term "person" includes one or more individuals, governments, governmental agencies, political subdivisions, labor unions, partnerships, associations, firms, mutual companies, corporations, companies, joint-stock companies, trusts, unincorporated organizations, societies, trustees, trustees in bankruptcy, or receivers;

(5) the term "employee" means any individual employed by an employer, any individual treated as an employee for purposes of the workers' compensation law of any State, and any employee who is employed by a State or a political subdivision thereof, except that such term shall not include any individual whose employment is covered by (a) subchapters I and II of chapter 81 of title 5, United States Code, (b) the Act entitled "An Act relating to the liability of common carriers by railroad to their employees in certain cases," approved April 22, 1908 (35 Stat. 65, 45 U.S.C. 51-60), (c) the Longshoremen's and Harbor Workers' Compensation Act (33 U.S.C. 901-950), or (d) section 20 of the Act entitled "An Act to remove certain burdens on the American merchant marine and encourage the American foreign carrying trade, and for other purposes," approved June 26, 1884 (46 U.S.C. 688) . . .

(7) an "injury" shall be deemed to have arisen out of and in the course of employment if work-related factors were a significant cause of the injury, and includes (a) any damage or harmful change in the human organism, which results in illness, disability, impairment, disfigurement, disease, or death, whether or not the result of an accident; (b) any damage or loss of prosthetic and corrective devices; (c) any injury caused by the willful act of a third person directed against an employee because of employment.

(8) the term "physician" includes surgeons, podiatrists, dentists, clinical psychologists, optometrists, chiropractors as specified in the Federal Employees' Compensation Act, (5 U.S.C. 8101 [2]), and osteopathic practitioners within the scope of their practice as defined by State law, and any other individual licensed to provide health care services reimbursable without referral from a physician under the workers' compensation law of any State;

(9) the term "disability" includes (A) incapacity to perform or obtain work suitable to the employee's qualifications and training; (B) incapacity to earn wages which the employee was receiving at the time of a work-related injury; or, (C) incapacity for future work and wages. . . .

Coverage and Venue

SEC. 4. (a) The provisions of this Act shall apply to all employers and all employees in any State.

(b) Whenever employment requires travel between States or between the United States and any other country, the injured employee or the survivors of such employee may claim benefits under the local State workers' compensation law as established pursuant to this Act—

(1) in the State of the employer's principal place of business; or

(2) in the State of the employer's headquarters; or

(3) in the State where the employee was hired, or accepted employment, or appointed, or elected; or

(4) in the State where the injury, disease, or death for which benefits are claimed occurred; or

(5) in the State in which the employee was domiciled at the time of the injury, death, or discovery or incidence of disease arising out of and in the course of employment.

Entitlement to Workers' Compensation Benefits

SEC. 5. Any employee who becomes disabled or dies due to any injury arising out of and in the course of employment, or the survivors of any employee whose death was due to any injury which arose out of and in the course of employment, shall be entitled to the following benefits notwithstanding any contrary provision of State law:

(a) compensation, medical benefits, rehabilitation services, and other benefits for disability or death which are provided under the law of the State having appropriate jurisdiction.

(b) An initial selection of a physician from among all physicians licensed by the State and approved by the State workers' compensation agency.

(c) No time or dollar maximum limitation on the total amount of compensation payable in case of death or total disability.

(d) No time or dollar maximum limitation on the type or extent of medical care, rehabilitation services, or other services (or expenses for such care or services) determined to be necessary by the State workers' compensation agency in any case.

(e) Compensation payable to injured workers for total disability or to survivors of a deceased employee under the workers' compensation law of that State not less than 66⅔ per centum of the employee's average weekly wage subject to the following limitations:

(1) During the one-year period which begins on the first day of the first calendar quarter which begins after two years after the date of the enactment of this Act, the maximum weekly benefits payable shall not be less than 100 per centum of the statewide average weekly wage during the first four of the last six calendar quarters.

(2) During the one-year period immediately following the one-year period for which maximum weekly benefits are prescribed under clause (1), the maximum weekly benefits payable shall be not less than 150 per centum of the statewide average weekly wage during the first four of the last six calendar quarters.

(3) During the one-year period immediately following the one-year period for which maximum weekly benefits are prescribed under clause (2), the maximum weekly benefits payable shall be not less than 200 per centum of the statewide average weekly wage during the first four of the last six calendar quarters.

(f) Minimum weekly compensation benefits for total disability under the workers' compensation law of that State during any one year period beginning July 1 and ending June 30 not less than 50 per centum of the statewide average weekly wage during the immediately preceding calendar year or the injured employee's actual weekly wage, whichever is less. The minimum weekly benefits in death cases under the workers' compensation law of that State during any one-year period beginning July 1 and ending June 30 shall be not less than 50 per centum of the statewide average weekly wage during the immediately preceding calendar year.

(g) Rehabilitation services to reduce disability and to restore the physical, psychological, social, and vocational functioning of the injured employee. Any injured employee undergoing a program of rehabilitation or receiving any rehabilitation services shall not have compensation benefits reduced while such rehabilitation is being received; such rehabilitation benefits are additional benefits and shall not be converted to or replace any other available compensation.

(h) Where an injury causes death, or an employee who is entitled to receive compensation for total permanent disability subsequently dies as a result of such compensable injury, death benefits under the workers' compensation law of that State payable to the deceased employee's widow or widowers for life until remarriage, with at least two years' benefits payable upon remarriage, and to surviving children until at least age eighteen (or age twenty-five if the surviving child is a full-time student in an accredited educational institution), or for life if any such surviving child is physically or mentally incapable of self-support at the time of the death of the employee provided the compensation will not continue if such child becomes capable of self-support. Such benefits are additional benefits and shall not be converted to or replace any compensation otherwise available.

(i) A waiting period for benefits under the workers' compensation law of that State not longer than three days and a period for qualifying for retroactive benefits during such waiting period not longer than fourteen days.

(j) Periodic adjustment, at least annually, of compensation benefits which are paid for incurred disability or death, to reflect increases in statewide average weekly wage levels and the benefit levels, or maximum limits thereon, provided under the workers' compensation law of that State.

(k) Reasonable attorney's fees added to an award under the workers' compensation law of that State when a claimant has succeeded in obtaining or increasing the award through adjudicatory proceedings at any stage of a controverted claim.

(l) (1) An original claim for compensation for disability or death under the workers' compensation law of that State may be filed within three years after the injury or death.

(2) In a case of latent disability, the time for filing claim under the workers' compensation law of that State shall not begin to run until the employee has a compensable disability and is aware, or by the exercise of reasonable diligence should have been aware, of the causal relationship of the compensable disability to the employment.

(3) The timely filing of a disability claim under the workers' compensation laws of that State because of injury will satisfy the time requirements for a death claim based on the same injury although the fact of death should be promptly communicated to the appropriate agency after its occurrence.

(4) The time limitations in paragraphs (1) and (2) do not—

(A) begin to run against a minor until that minor reaches 21 years of age or has had a legal representative appointed; or

(B) run against an incompetent individual while that individual is incompetent and has no duly appointed legal representative.

(m) Appropriate compensation even where an employee's religious beliefs do not permit the usual medical care or rehabilitation services to be utilized in the cure of injuries, diseases, and disabilities.

Employment Related Diseases

SEC. 6. (a). The Secretary of Health, Education, and Welfare is authorized and directed to undertake a study of diseases related to employment for the purposes of this Act and to make recommendations for appropriate standards for determining (1) whether such a disease arose out of and in the course of employment, and (2) whether death or disability was due to such disease. Such standards may include reasonable presumptions whenever appropriate. In carrying out the study required by this section, the Secretary of Health, Education, and Welfare shall consult with the Director of the National Institute of Occupational Safety and Health and such other organizations of employers and employees as are appropriate with respect to new diseases that are suspected of being employment related. The results of such study shall be published and distributed to the States, and shall be furnished to the Secretary of Labor.

(b) Whenever the Secretary of Labor determines on the basis of the study provided under subsection (a) of this section that new or additional standards should be promulgated for determining whether a disease arose out of and in the course of employment, or whether death or disability was due to such disease, such standards shall be referred to the Advisory Commission. Within two hundred and seventy days of such referral, the Advisory Commission shall inform the Secretary whether it approves, disapproves, or approves with modifications such standards. The Advisory Commission may also, on its own motion, recommend any such standards to the Secretary. The Secretary may promulgate any standard approved or recommended by the Advisory Commission (including any modifications so recommended). The promulgation of such standards shall be governed by the provisions of the Administrative Procedure Act (5 U.S.C. 551 et seq.). Any standard so promulgated shall be enforceable in any State as if such standard was included in the worker's compensation law of that State.

Cover and book design: Pat Taylor

DATE DUE

MAY 2 5 1981			
JUN 1 5 1981	OCT 1 3 '90		
OCT 3 1 1983			
MAY 2 8 1984			
SEP 1 0 1984	MAY 7		
FEB 11 '85			
NOV 11 '85			
NOV 11 '90			
APR 17 '91			
OCT 1 2 '93			
NOV 12 '93			
MAR 19 '97			
	261-2500		Printed in USA